on track ...

The Pretenders
1978-1990

every album, every song

Richard Butterworth

sonicbondpublishing.com

Sonicbond Publishing Limited
www.sonicbondpublishing.co.uk
Email: info@sonicbondpublishing.co.uk

First Published in the United Kingdom 2025
First Published in the United States 2025

British Library Cataloguing in Publication Data:
A Catalogue record for this book is available from the British Library

Copyright Richard Butterworth 2025

ISBN 978-1-78952-358-4

The right of Richard Butterworth to be identified
as the author of this work has been asserted by him
in accordance with the Copyright, Designs and Patents Act 1988.
All rights reserved. No part of this publication may be reproduced, stored in a
retrieval system or transmitted in any form or by any means, electronic, mechanical,
photocopying, recording or otherwise, without prior permission in writing from
Sonicbond Publishing Limited

Typeset in ITC Garamond Std & ITC Avant Garde Gothic
Printed and bound in England

Graphic design and typesetting: Full Moon Media

Acknowledgements

Thanks and due respect to all Pretenders past and present, passive or active, knowingly or not, for their invaluable help.

Most of all to Sue, with fond love, and no pretending.

on track ...
The Pretenders
1978-1990

Contents

Foreword 7
Introduction 9
Pretenders (1980) 33
Pretenders II (1981) 51
Learning To Crawl (1984) 68
Get Close (1986) 84
Packed! (1990) 104
Postscript 121

Foreword

On the following views and reviews, I should stress these reflect nothing other than the subjective self-importance of the author. If you've read *Jefferson Airplane On Track* and *Pink Floyd On Track*, both available from Sonicbond, you already know this. Nothing should be taken as holy writ, nor as the slightest hint that my acuity is in any way sharper than yours. Establishing the provenance and sequences of gigs, dates and recording sessions – and even the names of early Pretenders' collaborators now lost among back issues of *NME* – would test the principles of a Heisenberg; where there's uncertainty of some gravity, I've cravenly reported two (or more) conflicting versions in the hope that you, reader, will be exercised enough to discover the truth for yourself. Or, of course, that you know the truth already and you've immediately spotted me winging it. Talking of which, rather than setting out learned technical analyses of musical structure (of which my deeper knowledge is, I confess, rudimentary), I dwell on lyrical connotation and my emotional responses to The Pretenders' work. Everyone has their own take on the meanings of rock songs, and the frequent ambiguities of a Chrissie Hynde lyric can render all interpretations equally valid (or not at all, as is likely the case with mine). Incidentally, I'm not the first in print to make the Suzi Quatro connection, and kudos to Adam Sobsey for his observations in his excellent *Chrissie Hynde: A Musical Biography*. I promise mine arrived independently. (The validity of the Chrissie-Suzi axis did not escape Pete Farndon, as we'll see.)

Despite The Pretenders' admirable longevity, there was good reason to end this account in 1990 (although, again, this is a personal viewpoint that I should not expect every fan of the band to share). My position is this: by the end of the 1980s, a measure of doubt was inhibiting the ballsy rock 'n' roll creativity at which Ms Hynde and her cohort had proven themselves so adept. Although to Chrissie's credit, and our gain, she reconfigured the group and continued to make great music through the following decade and beyond, I felt the real Pretenders story was to be found earlier: Chrissie's Ohio adolescence and her arrival in 1973 London; the cultivation, and occasional renunciation, of the musicians, managers, movers and shakers on which the fickle and febrile 1970s British recording industry rolled; the exhaustive search for, and formation of, the original Pretenders; their earliest recording sessions; and the first 12 years of the band's existence, with all the trials, tribulations, truculence, tripwires and tragedy that tried hard, but never quite succeeded, to break up the band. In fashioning this narrative, I've taken a fine comb to the five studio albums created in that period, appraising each original's every song with suitable *On Track* rigour, together with some of the associated B-sides and deep cuts subsequently only to see the light of day on remastered CD packages. I have not, however, waded through every last rough demo or live reading to have been flooded into lavish, multi-disc box sets, mainly because I have more important things to acquire with the many multiples of 20 quid that such fancies usually cost. Especially given my compact disc shelves are already groaning under the collective weight of numerous issues of the same Pretenders records, in varying mystifying degrees of FLAC, Atmos and Lossless 5.1 Stereo.

Finally, my fond love and thanks for her forbearance to my partner, Sue, herself once a pretender, if a non-combatant.

Introduction

> It was kind of a do-it-yourself time and it was really not about musicianship, it was about personality and attitude.
> Chrissie Hynde, *The Guardian*, 2016

Within a year of its brief bout of insurrectionary Tourette's in 1976, history's most disorderly youth tribe was back inside the borstal. Punk's analogue, cloth-cap rage would be tenderised for at least a decade by the middle classes and their syndrums, big suits, dreadful haircuts and touching *arriviste* odes to consumerism. Although a few punks took a rightwards lurch to oi! (a sub-category residing mainly in pubs and on football terraces), it would take grunge, a similarly clannish interlude not so much openly hostile as nihilistically aimless, to later slouch in, claim the low ground and once again remind everyone what rock 'n' roll was supposed to do.

But early in 1978, punk's more immediate idiomatic successor wasn't quite ready to twist its coarse mother tongue around the tinctures of prog, Can and Beefheart that made post-punk the most intoxicating new music since krautrock. Somewhere along the line, The Pretenders swept in to occupy a greenfield site ripe for development, there to create a durable, upmarket estate of great songs built into the most potent commercial rock 'n' roll heard since the heyday of The Rolling Stones.

Today, a fresh batch of those songs can still fuel a fire that, like The Stones', ought to have been quenched long ago. Studios will be booked, accomplices hired and the dark arts of rehearsals, recording, mixdown and marketing will grind into action. There might be a supporting tour, the odd global pandemic permitting. Finally, another album arrives accredited to The Pretenders, even if the galaxy of collaborators pretending to be Pretenders – some stellar sessioneers, others little known prior to their appointment – really orbit a single, universal constant: the force of nature that is Chrissie Hynde.

The American expat was forming her idealised 'motorcycle gang with guitars' in London just as punk finished urinating in its last few telephone boxes. Today, often AWOL but never officially declared lost, The Pretenders continue to balance in an apparent state of flux, their founder, rhythm guitarist, singer and principal songwriter continually remaking and remodelling her group according to creative urge and circumstance. If Robert Fripp saw in King Crimson 'less a group, more a way of doing things' – the guitarist's typically gnomic way of saying that art can only flourish if the means to make it is constantly renewed – the conceit equally can be applied to The Pretenders: less a group, perhaps, more a nebulous lifeforce which, since 1978, has blended and reshaped angry punk, crunching rock and chartworthy, elegant, sublimely intelligent pop.

Despite the odd solo venture, the band have never traded as 'Chrissie Hynde'. Nor were they ever, at least nominally, Chrissie Hynde and 'her' Pretenders. From the beginning, industry insiders weighed her up for solo stardom. Unsurprisingly they saw in the pale, slender, charismatic Ohioan a sure route to a satisfyingly black balance sheet (a theoretically happy situation the eager tenderfeet were obliged to deal with even before the release of their second album). But Chrissie was having none of it. Her objective was to be first among equals in the last gang in town, the individual absorbed by the collective but never suppressed by it, even as fortune, innate talent and ball-breaking chutzpah embedded her as nothing less than a natural, if unwilling, leader.

The Pretenders fruited as a tight, empathetic quartet in the classic mould. The lineup of singer/rhythm guitarist, lead guitarist, bassist and drummer arrived fully formed: good looks, great hair, an instinctive grasp of rock's foundational, elegantly-wasted rebel ethos. They were bolshie and sexy and conversant with the ideal angle of incidence of a mid-slung Telecaster (the journeyman, single-cut forerunner of the curvaceous Strat would become welded to Chrissie Hynde, much as it did Bruce Springsteen, Steve Cropper, Rick Parfitt and other similarly no-nonsense stars). The Pretenders had a barrowful of attitude and, unlike many me-too outriders clogging up the scene in the wake of the great Damned-Pistols-Clash UK punk offensive, were rounded off with the musical chops to support it. The cheery, Beatley nonchalance of The Pretenders' men defused their reluctant mama's resentful glower, while the whole band strutted like roosters on a dungheap and burned more high-test than a V8 Mustang at Pomona. Part-Mose Allison, part-Stones, part-Beatles, part-James Brown, part-Dylan, part-Ronnie Spector: what could possibly go wrong?

Within four years and the first brace of albums, however, agencies measurably darker than the caprices of the band's founder had imposed savage change. Narcotic misadventure took bassist Pete Farndon (whose calamitous heroin habit led to his dismissal in 1982 and his death a year later) and guitarist James Honeyman-Scott (who suffered a terminal, opioid-related heart attack two days after Farndon was sacked). Both did what they did well, Honeyman-Scott in particular; one day, he'd be tagged as a key influence. In an online interview, ex-Smith Johnny Marr, who'd later do his own hard yards with The Pretenders, alluded to Jimmy's mastery of the 'jingle-jangle' guitar sound (usually derived from a 12-string Rickenbacker) with which The Beatles, The Searchers and The Byrds invented folk-rock:

> [Jimmy] was the last important influence on my playing before I went out on my own. The first time I played 'Kid' with The Pretenders, I couldn't believe it. I've used that solo to warm up with every day for years.

More to the point – for at heart this was down-and-dirty rock 'n' roll purpose-built to frighten the horses – Farndon and Honeyman-Scott were closer aligned to their boss's witheringly fuck-you attitude than any one of their successors. The losses were keenly felt. The steel that Chrissie Hynde and her cohort forged from the molten pig-iron of British punk seemed like a one-off: four musicians in such exquisite balance that to lose one, never mind two, was bound to upset a fragile ecosystem. Imagine McCartney and Harrison quitting The Beatles in 1964, or The Doors mislaying Ray Manzarek and Robby Krieger after the release of *Strange Days*: of course, the surviving talent would have prospered, but the extraction of elements crucial to both bands' structural chemistries would have left neither quite the same again. As potent a creative lead as a Lennon or a Morrison, Hynde would continue to write and perform plenty of fine music without mothballing The Pretenders as a brand. But in their abrasive, take-no-prisoners prime, The Pretenders were a two-album deal and no more. As Chrissie and the last of the original four – drummer Martin Chambers – struggled to process the double tragedy, a third album came as a welcome and brilliantly surprising bonus by, effectively, a new band. The demise of the original lineup, however, ironically marked the start of the journey to *de facto* solo stardom Hynde never sought; a trek whose destination was assured before the 1980s were out and this narrative reaches its conclusion.

The first album, *Pretenders*, was a near-perfect 50-minute précis of the band's manifesto: acidic, confrontational lyrics, in places evoking an autobiographical Ohio, set in rousing rock lashed to chart-busting pop, the format superficially conventional. Yet while the album's creators were identifiably a dashing, well-fortified rock 'n' roll band yeasted with pop sensibilities, alkaline departures off-piste suggested a dominant paradigm was waiting to be upset whenever Chrissie sat down to write. Her casual take on compositional orthodoxy lent her songs numerous eccentric changes, with lyrical bonuses sometimes shoehorned into a stanza's back end as if to test the mettle of her rhythm section. No question, though, that these structural anomalies were eminent floor-fillers, even if tapping your feet required the immediate growth of several more.

Pretenders II, rush-made as the addictive personalities within the newly successful group were near-felled by drugs, fame and post-touring stress disorder, was a superb and logical successor, doing sterling service to build on the information set out in the maiden statement. Hynde's talents for an incisive lyric were developing nicely, setting up a gallery of vignetted, sharply truthful character studies whisked into similarly unconventional structures and metres. But more difficult times lay ahead; a third album, post-Jimmy, post-Pete, needed to regain an initiative which the double tragedy ought to have burned off. That *Learning To Crawl* succeeded so splendidly eulogises the tenacity of the surviving original members, not to mention Chrissie Hynde's shrewd choices in new collaborators.

By 1986, any notion that the fortunes of The Pretenders did not lie solely in the gift of a totemic focal point was starting to look fanciful; witness the fourth album's extensive team of hired hands. Not only did *Get Close* position Chrissie as the band's unquestionable leader, mentor and den mother, but the gnarly irregularities so crucial to The Pretenders' unwritten original doctrine were smoothed out, the leader dealing with loss while her maturity as a writer occasionally felt compromised. The songs remained crowd-pleasers, though, in a setting that was now shinily professional, rinsed in the fashionably pasteurised production values that their earthier, more artisanal predecessors eschewed. Maturity isn't always a desirable property in a down 'n' dirty rock band, but The Pretenders were now way beyond that, bringing in session accompaniment and two of the era's go-to producers, Steve Lillywhite and Bob Clearmountain, to replace the ever-reliable Chris Thomas. *Get Close* remains a fine collection of glossy, if occasionally shallow, 1980s funk-pop. Three years later, *Packed!*, the decade's final Pretenders album and the last discussed here, superficially suggested bagginess. For some it represented a lifeless drift from original values. Yet the album proved a grower, despite Chrissie's lyrics occasionally smacking of discontent and even self-pity. This was fair, perhaps, given her recent divorce and the fact that the 39-year-old was far from the voracious cougar suggested by journalists finding themselves on her wrong side. The album's tranche of crisp, polished pop songs largely lost the funk element, while benefiting from producer Mitchell Froom's canny avoidance of the 1980s digital production overload which in places weighed down *Packed!*'s predecessor.

Despite her high profile and obvious player-manager credentials, Chrissie Hynde has continued to resist the contention that she catalysed a shift from rock's male hegemony. Her remedy for the emancipation of the 'rock chick' was simple and direct, as she offered *Guitar*'s Huw Baines in 2021: 'You just tell [the rock patriarchy] to go fuck themselves. Problem solved.'

With Chambers the only other original member (even he was temporarily sidelined in 1986 due, according to the drummer, to Hynde's newly explicit leadership aspirations and consequent personnel clearances), the gang has rolled on as The Pretenders. Their identity has remained at one with a boss who's done more than most, if unintentionally, to encourage and empower women to front rock bands. Shirley Manson, Sheryl Crow, Delores O'Riordan, P. J. Harvey, Siouxsie Sioux, Joan Jett, Courtney Love and many others were always destined to shatter a once-impregnable XY glass ceiling. No matter her reluctance to don a mentor's mantle, Chrissie Hynde was their pioneer, facilitator and flagbearer. And she was nothing new, as she told *Rolling Stone*'s Kurt Loder in 1980:

> You've always had women playing instruments in the modern world. There's nothing butch about me. See, that's the big myth, you know – the 'loudmouthed American.' I am the loudmouthed American. No-one can be meaner, and no-one can be more of a cunt than I am. But I don't want to be. It's a front, you know? I just do what I do to get what I have to get.

Chrissie advised *The Guardian* in 2016:

> I am very grateful to punk because I was a girl, and I felt like if I got in a band, I'd be kind of a novelty act, but punk was all about non-discrimination. No-one cared because it was punk, so, you know, anyone could do anything they wanted.

It's surprising that Chrissie, who from almost the moment she arrived was drifting around London in leather miniskirts, torn denim and dead men's waistcoats, was never considered a bonafide punk – in the Damned-Pistols-Poly Styrene sense, anyway. The anomaly was pondered by her friend, guitarist Chris Spedding:

> Although she was certainly one of [punk's] instigators, Chrissie was too much of an individual, too much of a rebel, to get totally into that scene. But she was one of the first people to have that look. Yet, as soon as something became clearly defined, she'd rebel against it, which was the case with her and punk in the end.

Before the punkische disturbances of late 1976, and The Pretenders' arrival around 18 months later, relatively few women involved with otherwise male groups made convincing role models for the fledgling rocker from the Heartlands. Women had flourished as solo artists and as members of vocal groups that were often industry-built, The Ronettes, The Crystals, The Supremes and The Shangri-Las kicking open the door for the still more confected, but far less talented, Spice Girls, Sugababes, Pussycat Dolls and Girls Aloud. Rarer still were the instrumental bands whose distractingly all-female membership tended, in pop's dark ages, to trigger the chauvinist disdain today still aimed at ladies' football teams and women chief constables. Fanny, Goldie & The Gingerbreads, The Ace of Cups and She Trinity absorbed the mockery in order that, years later, The Slits, The Go-Gos, The Bangles and The Runaways wouldn't have to. But if she found herself part of a male-dominated guitars-keys-bass-drums setup, a woman was rarely the boss, unlikely to exert influence over the proper rock 'n' roll owned by the hard boys. As the industry clung to flyblown prejudices – quoted by *Melody Maker*'s Rob Partridge with commendable distaste in 1973 was this unattributed, cave-dwelling humdinger: 'the only constructive female role in the history of the music has been that of the fan' – the girlies were meant to know their place, even if it was just front-of-house eye candy.

As Chrissie Hynde hinted, a female instrumentalist adrift in a sea of testosterone was largely held to occupy a subordinate, mildly aberrant role, a symbol to attract press and talk. From the mid-1960s, a few equal partners emerged: trumpeter Cynthia Robinson and keyboardist Rose Stone were crucial contributors to Sly & The Family Stone, whose pathfinding, multiracial, multi-gender profile felt bravely different in 1966. Years before Fleetwood Mac could afford the best divorce lawyers, Christine McVie (née Perfect) won respect as singer/pianist with the plain, dirty old Mac's 1960s British blues-boom classmates Chicken Shack. In New York City, Maureen Tucker stood at her drumkit, flailing away at repetitive, genre-defining beats for The Velvet Underground. In an era of high idealism, these groups were notionally 'underground'; any ambition for chart success was scorned, both by the hip commentariat and, even if they quietly coveted the expensive drugs and Corvette Stingrays of stardom, many of the bands themselves. Despite Perfect's commanding execution of the Etta James-penned 1969 hit 'I'd Rather Go Blind', Chicken Shack never ranked beyond honest jobbers, remaining firmly rooted in the manly soil of the British provincial blues club. I'll leave the reader to ponder how frequently the Velvets' overdriven, feedback-soaked paeans to smack, sulphate and S&M troubled the 1967 pop charts.

Today it's impossible to quantify how many young women were moved to explore rock as a career by two particular 1960s British musicians: Essex hairdresser-turned-drummer Anne 'Honey' Lantree, whose band The Honeycombs scored an international hit in 1964 with producer Joe Meek's ringing stomper 'Have I The Right'; and Megan Davies, bassist with The Honeycombs' West Midlands peers The Applejacks, who took Brumbeat to the top ten for the first time with 'Tell Me When'. Media bellyaching followed these abnormalities in predictably short order: the era's confused, pre-internet trolls could care less that Lantree and Davies were decent, inspiring musicians. But at least there was someone to make the sandwiches.

As the Woodstock Nation fostered a new meritocracy, female lead or co-lead singers remained a novel minority. Surrounded by the fractious male monoliths of Jefferson Airplane, Grace Slick oozed vocal and compositional brilliance and unbridled charisma. Yet this cerebral ice queen, often lead singer but never leader, had five combative alphas to contend with. Airplane's personnel model was aped by numerous groups post-Summer of Love, especially in Britain; male-dominated rhythm machines from Pentangle to Fairport Convention were now fronted by ethereal hippie chicks with long, straight hair, gypsy skirts and voices, *pace* Collins, Baez et al, of mezzo-soprano purity. But a growing indulgence for sprawling jams was fuelling a sense of redundancy among non-playing vocalists. Short of guitar props, many were reduced to self-consciously hand-jiving at the mic while the men did the real graft. Celia Humphris, singer with the British folk-rock quintet Trees, was lost in space whenever her bandmates took off on extended flights of mansplaining electric guitar; Eclection's Kerrilee Male, a superb chanteuse underused by instrumentalists who'd subsequently find fame with better-known groups, gave up and sped back to obscurity in her native Australia; and one night at the Speakeasy, as Fairport's teenage guitar prodigy Richard Thompson soared off on a torrential awayday with Jimi Hendrix, vocalist Judy Dyble famously sat alone at the front of the stage, knitting.

Loosening social standards of the early 1970s brought spirit, confidence and female assertiveness. Feline and predatory, Maggie Bell (Stone The Crows), Elkie Brooks (Vinegar Joe) and Janita Haan (Babe Ruth) channelled Janis Joplin in whisky-permeated raunch as they prowled around the Marquee stage, all looking and sounding as if they smoked their male co-workers in a post-gig doobie every night of the week. If everyone in the band was happy to muck in with the domestics – a (male) bassist making the tea wasn't a given if it could be left to a girl, and posterity has proven the theoretically enlightened mores of 1970s pop culture to be largely fictional – all three women were reliant for musical direction respectively on founding guitarists Les Harvey, Pete Gage and Alan Shacklock. And Janis herself, hard-rocking and Southern Comfort-necking, overly anxious to be liked, was no bandleader; cut loose as a solo from Big Brother & The Holding Company, her neediness rotted to a sad, smack-fuelled demise. The New York poet Patti Smith, near enough in rockist insolence when she fronted her own, undeniably cooking Patti Smith Group, was too close to the Big Apple-Warholian intellectual twilight zone to entirely convince as a rock 'n' roll everywoman.

Elsewhere, the dangerous sexuality of Curved Air's Sonja Kristina was gleefully appropriated to publicise the band, the London listings mag *Time Out* habitually running photos of the singer without her top (to the disgust of women's libbers and the delight of the mainly male fans of the Vivaldi-mad proggers). Another progressive group with similarly neo-classical leanings was Renaissance, whose singer Annie Haslam's five-octave soprano range, along with the floaty gowns she resolutely kept on, radiated more Mother Earth than Babalon Moonchild. Though both vocalists were charismatic and hugely talented, their music was radioactive to the punks (although you sensed that Sonja, should she have chosen, easily could have held her own against Team Testosterone in a rock 'n' roll pissing contest).

But even the most original rock music and its architects are hybrid consequences of an expansive, ever-shifting network of human capital. Undoubtedly the ground was prepared for the young gun from Ohio by many more female artists of stature, from Sandy Denny to Miquette Giraudy, Kate Bush to Jacqui McShee, Bobbie Gentry to Joni Mitchell. This said, consider the story of a fellow Midwesterner, older by just over a year, who was once part of a full-on, all-female rock 'n' roll group and whose personal and career paths were spookily similar to Chrissie Hynde's.

Suzi Quatro was born in Detroit in 1950. The daughter of a jazz musician, at 14 she was singing and playing bass in a rock band, The Pleasure Seekers, with her sisters Patti and Arlene and their friends Nancy and Mary-Lou Ball. Honing their stagecraft alongside macho Detroit stars such as Bob Seger and Ted Nugent, The Pleasure Seekers quickly proved as Motor City-tough as any of their male peers short of the fearsome MC5. In 1968 the band signed with Mercury Records, becoming one of the earliest all-female rock groups to close a major-label deal. Then in 1971, the bassist and singer was talent-spotted by

Mickie Most, a powerful producer-arranger who would also guide the careers of Hot Chocolate, Smokie and The Sweet. Most relocated her to England in time for the glamrock gold-rush part-initiated by the Rak Records label boss. As even the plug-ugliest British plasterers suddenly lit themselves up in Max Factor and Revlon, Suzi turned out a string of wickedly commercial singles formulated on high rotation by Most and songwriting hits factory Nicky Chinn and Mike Chapman. It was a glitzy period of quasi-rock 'n' roll, the venerable form reimagined with cocked managerial eyebrows and mountainous drifts of pancake. Wizzard, The Rubettes and Alvin Stardust delivered retro-nouveau parodies of Presley, Holly, Berry and Spector, while the nation's teens, bedecked in scoop-necked t-shirts, bell-bottomed dungarees and six-inch platform clogs, tottered awkwardly to Suzi's pop-rock chugalugs 'Can The Can', '48 Crash' and 'Devil Gate Drive'.

Yet like Chrissie Hynde, Elvis fan Suzi had proper rock 'n' roll coming out of her ears. Clad head-to-toe in black leather and so slight her monstrous Gibson EB2 bass hid her like a Zulu shield, she had bad attitude aplenty and did reliably good interview, unblushingly enthusing about her love of rock and the thrill of generating its lowest notes via the 'throb of the huge instrument between my legs'. Though no Pretenders, Suzi's band proved an amiably meat 'n' potatoes, workingman's foil to the boss's brash, flash Motor City sassiness. She was no ingenue or coquettish functionary: the image was blunt, tomboyish, greasy, in charge, a bona fide bandleader. Suzi could as easily have spent her adolescence tinkering beneath an oil sump at a Detroit auto plant as dating the high-school jock.

Yet despite her old dues-paying days with The Pleasure Seekers and the fact that, even now, this was one tough broad who could happily match her brawny colleagues shot for shot, Suzi never escaped pop's middle of the road, prevented by her people and the dead hand of the recording establishment from allowing whatever truly rebellious instincts she had to flower. Circumspection blocked Quatro from stealing an early march on the young woman who would make cocky, bedenimed rock 'n' roll unisex a fine art. 'The sort of things Suzi Quatro was supposed to be,' mused Pete Farndon in 1981, 'Chrissie actually was.'

Christine Ellen Hynde was born on 7 September 1951 in Akron, Ohio. Her father, Melville, was a manager for Ohio Bell. Her mother, Delores, was a secretary and an ex-model. Music was in the family; her older brother, Terry, played alto saxophone and would form a group in 1968 called The Numbers Band. Christine's first kiss was a boozy slobber from soul giant Jackie Wilson at a 1965 concert. Gifted a copy of The Kinks' first album the same year, Christine tentatively took up guitar, accompanying 'Stop Your Sobbing'; Ray Davies' song would become her future band's maiden single and her own conduit to the head Kink's romantic affections. At 16, her musical ability rudimentary, she began writing songs.

In 2023 she would tell *The Guardian* what motivated her as a writer:
I don't even think of myself as a songwriter or even a musician. I just feel as if I'm doing my thing, and I've got away with it. I started writing because I wasn't good enough to play along to the radio and I was too shy to play with the guys in my high school. I had to write my own tunes, so I had something to play when I was learning my baritone ukulele.

Given her famous self-belief, it's surprising Chrissie felt too shy to seek gigs with the local dudes and their garage bands. But young women in mid-1960s rock groups were rarely taken seriously – least of all by adenoidal punks in Akron. Even she might have ended up fetching the milk and cookies.

By May 1970, Chrissie was studying art at Kent State University when the National Guard shot dead four protesting but unarmed fellow students, a close friend's boyfriend among them. The outrage was marked by Neil Young in his hit song 'Ohio'. When David Bowie played Cleveland in 1972, Chrissie and a friend talked their way into the Spiders' suite and took Ziggy Stardust himself to dinner in her mother's Oldsmobile. Although she was a massive fan, her admiration for Bowie (and for Davies, irrespective of what lay ahead) was eclipsed by her worship of the man who would come to define everything she found most dangerously alluring about rock 'n' roll. She told *Guitar*:

I didn't become a mad-keen Iggy Pop fan till I discovered David Bowie. I saw the first gig that David did in the States when he came to Ohio – I was at the soundcheck. He really got me refocused.

Her playlist of the time included Iggy & The Stooges, Young, Lou Reed, Tim Buckley, Sly Stone, Jimi Hendrix, James Brown, The Chambers Brothers and Paul Butterfield. Yet other desires were gaining traction, Bowie's flat London estuary vowels providing a clue to their origin. As she put it in her memoir, *Reckless*: 'We were the Love Generation, especially if an English accent was incorporated.'

For the teenager growing up in 'Boredsville, USA', the local talent paled beside the skinny, libidinous British singers and guitarists touring the US in the wake of The Beatles. The Fab Four's Stateside triumph in 1964 inspired similar success for The Rolling Stones, The Animals, The Kinks, Dave Clark Five, Them, Herman's Hermits and Manfred Mann. The reaction to these pushy limeys of every American youth with three chords and a vacant stare was to occupy his old man's garage and form The Standells, The Count Five, The Seeds, or many another early US punk band. By 1967 a second wave of British marauders was continuing to return America's own music with interest and extra feedback, looping classic roots R&B back on itself and dispatching the thunderous results from towering Marshall stacks. Hotelkeepers the breadth of the Union nailed down their TV sets as The Jeff Beck Group, The Who, Cream, The Yardbirds and other ruffians hit the cities and the Jack

Daniels and detonated cherry bombs in the soft furnishings. America had lost its virginity; well-hung with snow-white tan, the British had well and truly come: 'We had no sexual experience,' Chrissie wrote, 'but we had Robert Plant.' As she told Kurt Loder in 1980:

> I was never too interested in high school. I mean, I never went to a dance. I never went on a date and never went steady. It became pretty awful for me. Except, of course, I could go see bands and that was the kick. I used to go to Cleveland to see any band. So I was in love a lot of the time, but mostly with guys in bands who I had never met. For me, knowing that Brian Jones was out there – or later that Iggy Pop was out there – made it kind of hard for me to get too interested in the boys around me. I had bigger things in mind.

In a Cleveland hotel room in 1966, Chrissie and her friend Cindy Smith met Rod Stewart and Ron Wood, then touring with Jeff Beck. The audience was brokered by Nemo, a local deejay pal. Despite fronting the trio's entry fee (a bag of weed), Nemo was soon cashiered, the subsequent entertainment limited to a congenial smoke between the two teenagers and their only slightly older predators. (Rod would later write and record 'Cindy's Lament' and 'Cindy Incidentally', respectively as a solo and with The Faces; while it's unclear whether either is about Ms Smith, the obvious long-term regrets of young women who'd avoided falling into the sack with the old goat probably became a rich songwriting seam.) As Chrissie told *Rolling Stone*:

> I'm not trying to put this on, but I seriously didn't know what was going on. I was a real virgin, man. I didn't even know what it was. And I just looked, and I said, 'I can't stay here tonight. I've gotta take my driver's training course in the morning. Let's go!' I insisted on leaving because I wanted to get my driver's license. It never occurred to me until years later what could have transpired that night, you know? Just think, Ronnie Wood would've been my first big one.

Akron, the 27th largest city in the US, could never be considered a great American rock 'n' roll proving ground. San Francisco produced Jefferson Airplane and Los Angeles the Byrds: Akron made airships. If New York City was the petri dish for The Velvet Underground's composites of hard drugs and sexual fetish, the real Rubber City was the Midwest home of tyre manufacturers Goodyear and Firestone. Hynde aside, little rock 'n' roll has risen from the town other than The Black Keys, The Waitresses, Ruby & The Romantics and Devo (whose Mark Mothersbaugh played with Chrissie in his early band Sat. Sun. Mat.). And while Pere Ubu, The Isley Brothers, Nine Inch Nails and Bootsy Collins all hailed from Ohio – the author must here also cede the floor to The McCoys, the loutish quartet answerable for that joyously brainless punk ur-text 'Hang On Sloopy' – for some sons of the prairies, such as Dave Grohl and Joe Walsh, it would take a trek to the west coast to find fame and fortune.

For others, the signpost to rock 'n' roll immortality pointed east. Determined to leave, Chrissie saved $1,000 from waiting tables and other casual work. In May 1973, she sold her Ovation guitar and, with Cindy, flew to London. Despite her initial dismay that Tony Orlando & Dawn, not The Stones, were top of the UK charts, she found employment selling plastic handbags at Centre Point market. She observed:

> Lank-haired guys with seedy complexions wearing short, brown leather bomber jackets with lousy collars; girls in flowered dresses and wavy, nondescript haircuts that owed nothing to Vidal Sassoon. It looked like the sixties had been hijacked by the Amish.

Due to a post-midnight ban on alcohol and male companionship, Bayswater's Lion Court Hotel asked the two Americans to leave. Cindy decoupled, while Chris rented a room in a Clapham flat courtesy of a neighbouring stallholder. Lacking retail acumen, she was sacked from the market after a few days, then her Fine Art degree landed her a job as a runner at a firm of architects for £17 per week . After the freeways and shopping malls of Akron, London felt refreshingly lo-fi; Chris revelled in the tube and the buses and not having to wait to be collected by friends with cars.

She'd travelled light, arriving in the UK with little more than a toothbrush and three items that were genuinely indispensable: the Velvet Underground's *White Light/White Heat* and Iggy & The Stooges' *Raw Power* and *Fun House*. The LPs were stolen not long after her arrival, the loss and natural sense of displacement causing Chris briefly to consider returning to Ohio. At a house party in west London she lamented her losses to anyone who'd listen. Up piped Nick Kent, a journalist on the weekly *New Musical Express*: 'I know Iggy.'

As an early-1970s London chat-up line, this was of limited value. With The Stooges, Iggy Pop had been the talk of the American Midwest since 1967. Alongside fellow Michiganians The MC5, they'd forged a reputation among local hipsters for incendiary live shows, the guitar-driven, paint-stripping ferocity of both groups torching any misconception that punk would one day all be the result of a stray remark by Malcolm McLaren. In 1973 Britain, however, the wider rock audience was still some years from anointing Pop as the official Godfather of Punk, despite positive underground rumblings and, in an October 1972 Stooges review for English *Cream* magazine, Kent's prescient celebration of Iggy as 'the Punk Messiah of the Teenage Wasteland'. Chris had a few reservations about her new home: the inferiority of British rock radio, lousy coffee, the fact that she had not yet come across someone with similar Iggy proclivities. But here was this 'emaciated oddball

19

in leather jeans, sporting a tooth earring, Keith Richards style', who knew his rock music and, crucially, appeared to carry an access-all-areas pass to the zeitgeist. And, shit, he knew Iggy. He'd even written the *NME* article – his first for the paper – which convinced the American that England was the place for any proto-rocker to be. Nick talked her into letting him crash at her Clapham flat. (Chris claims that he moved in within a week, although according to his 2010 memoir, *Apathy For The Devil*, Nick waited a respectful two months to be invited.)

The relationship briefly gleamed, Nick squiring Chris around the many venues at which the reporter enjoyed virtual backstage loyalty cards. The duo cut a glamorous, raggedly-damaged swathe through London bohemia: she the rock-mad American neophyte hungrily mopping up the swinging sixties' early-1970s leftovers; he the pale, rail-thin English Stones wannabe, his guitar talents way short of sometime drug-buddy Keith Richards, but who could pen discursive articles about the music in seductively dreamy streams of gonzo consciousness. One night in a pub, as Hynde put it in her memoir:

> I went off on one about some band or other in front of a long-haired intellectual type across the table, a friend of Nick's. The guy leaned forward and said, 'You should write for us.' Nick introduced me to him. [It was] Ian MacDonald, his assistant editor.

Following a maiden piece joyfully trashing Neil Diamond and a session spent discussing porn with Brian Eno (she spent part of it hanging upside-down dressed as a dominatrix), Chris began filing hip, quirkily entertaining gig reviews and profiles, ruffling the feathers of orthodox rock journalism for £30 per article. Among them was a piece on Suzi Quatro, the fruits of an interview in the ladies' room at the Reading Festival. Although her later take on her period as a journo was typically sclerotic – they hired 'any old Tom, Dick or Harry off the street with a big mouth to write for them' – she now had the opportunity to laud her heroes in print, with a little inkwell of vitriol set aside for those she fingered as the period's more complacent acts. The author remembers her *NME* columns as spiky, feisty and often very funny, but such enthusiasm was not shared by Chris, who later dismissed her scribbling as 'half-baked philosophical drivel'. Possibly as a by-product of the hate mail generated by her salty reflections, she was adored by a paper now firmly on a track that had begun with sly satire and would soon arrive at sulphurous, often vicious iconoclasm. Unafraid to poke at pop's mainstream deities – 'all four Neil Diamond fans in Britain wanted me dead' – what she would ridicule as nonsensical tirades became early matrices for Julie Burchill and the other urban guerrillas priming their editorial AK47s in *NME*'s newsroom. Chrissie would later sell her typewriter to Burchill for £17; as a valedictory comment on her brief career as a rock scribe, she was 'passing on the baton of how to fuck off the nation and get paid for it.' Meanwhile, her *NME* stint gave oxygen to a brand:

[Later, I was] introduced to people as Chrissie, either because Chris was a guy's name in Limeytown or because Nick preferred Chrissie. The 'flourish' came off Hynde (a thinly veiled ruse on my part to throw the Home Office). Thus, I became Chrissie Hynd of the *NME* and no-one called me Chris ever again.

Reborn, Chrissie was keen to distance herself from a craft to which she, if no-one else, believed her skills were ill-suited. She quit after *NME* editor Nick Logan requested a retrospective piece on The Velvet Underground. Though a committed Velvets fan, she knew it was time to go: 'I didn't want to look back.'

Her departure coincided with the rise of two waspish influencers, effectively recruiting sergeants for a threatening new youth movement. Malcolm McLaren and Vivienne Westwood ran a King's Road boutique called Let It Rock, later Too Fast To Live, Too Young To Die. They sold drape jackets, brothel-creepers, drainpipe strides and other retro clobber, their customers a mixture of glam-rockers and rock 'n' roll-purist motorbike greasers. Chrissie sometimes stopped by with Nick in Let It Rock days; the shop was still selling ironic winkle-pickers when the owners hired her as a sales assistant. Tired of the violent posturing of their mainly Teddy Boy clientele, always on the lookout for a new public moral outrage, McLaren and Westwood cooked up another makeover scheme.

If the boutique's earlier brand identities suited its relatively innocent merchandise, the new name – SEX – left little doubt about the apparel behind its 4ft-high pink latex fascia. The shop was now apparently transplanted from the clip-joints of Soho. Passing Chelsea hipsters weren't so much enticed as yanked on dog chains into a gothic Hades of S&M slave collars, ankle restraints, nipple clamps, safety-pinned fetish trousers and torn t-shirts depicting swastikas, gay cowboys and similarly lurid definers of the coming punk ethos. Much of this exotica was distressed or designed by McLaren and Westwood (who was fast turning into punk's own Norman Hartnell) and SEX became London's most fashionably edgy place to chill out and be seen. Among early customers, hangers-on and occasional assistants were four scallies who'd soon comprise the original Sex Pistols – among them the 'teenaged west London delinquent, Steve Jones', with whom Chrissie may have had a fling just as her relationship with Nick was boiling over – along with such other colourful pre-infamy punklings as Jordan, Siouxsie Sioux, Helen of Troy, Steven Severin and Adam Ant.

The SEX connection, and the stimuli of the surprisingly temperate, 'genuine English eccentrics' McLaren and Westwood, were more milestones on Chrissie's journey into the British rock 'n' roll underbelly. The job wasn't to last. Possibly for good reason, Nick became convinced of his now ex-girlfriend's infidelity. One day the well-refreshed writer stormed into the shop and, as McLaren hid under a table, attempted brain surgery on Chrissie with a studded leather belt. She noted in *Reckless*:

[Nick] was cross with me for dumping him... a local guy who'd been sitting quietly in the corner stood up and knocked Kent out... [he] was sprawled out on his back, tooth knocked out, unconscious long enough for me to step over him and run out the shop.

The smarter Cheyne Walk freeholders were now relying on SEX for their party packs of bespoke whips and gimp masks, so the violent irony might have passed Chrissie's employers by. 'The next day, Viv said they didn't need me anymore,' she wrote. 'I guess they didn't want some wacko trashing the place because of me.' (For balance, I'm obliged to report Nick's slightly differing account: promising rapprochement and 'a new beginning', Chrissie called to suggest they meet at the shop and go out together. By the following day, she'd pivoted, acidly advising Nick that she had acquired a new boyfriend, adding a departing 'go fuck yourself' for good measure. Nick, who like his now undeniably ex-paramour enjoyed a hearty appetite for Class As, has not disputed the belt.)

Bouncing from SEX, Chrissie was soon on the move thanks to another colourful local. Flipos, a fellow drinker at the fashionable King's Road pub The Roebuck, invited her to sing in a band he was forming in Paris. Chrissie needed travel funds, so she talked her way past the receptions of three recording companies (announcing herself as Chrissie Hynd of the *NME*), subsequently selling her swag of album review copies to a second-hand record shop in Soho.

According to *Reckless*, Chrissie's Parisian experience was a picaresque, late-20th-century retread of La Belle Époque: a potpourri of poets, posers, losers, musos, artists, gamblers, low lives, cross-dressers, cabaret dancers, Montparnasse chancers and La Coupole fashionistas; everything short of Pablo Picasso and, more to the point, the band. After Flipos installed her in a small house near the Eiffel Tower, Chrissie was introduced to Sasha Letronière, the phantom group's proposed singer. Sasha invited Chrissie to live in an apartment which the Dutch-Chinese scenester shared with her 'husband/wife' Sabrina: by day a Lou Reed leatherboy lookalike; by night tricked out in feathers and sequins for a cabaret drag spot at L'Alcazar.

The flat was a blend of minimalist austerity and bohemian fantasy. Spartan furniture was set off by silken Moroccan wall hangings, purportedly relocated from the set of the infamously decadent Mick Jagger vehicle, *Performance*. Chrissie briefly dated a 35-year-old Afghani professional poker player: a fellow Hendrix fan, committed night-owl and dawn habitue of bars on Boulevard Raspail, there regularly to breakfast on sugar cubes dunked in whisky. Sasha gifted Chrissie a Japanese Les Paul copy, but the thrilling rock 'n' roll future promised by the 'mad urchin and homeless gypsy' Flipos was looking redundant. She instead hooked up with two Keith Richards clones, a venture that in turn failed for want of a drummer. Further misfires followed, as Chrissie recounted in *Reckless*:

It didn't take long to see that nothing was going to come together in a madhouse. No-one spoke English, which was a problem because they all wanted to sound like The Rolling Stones, who were at the height of their 'elegantly wasted' period.

She recorded that her time with Sasha and Sabrina was the most enjoyable of her young life – 'I was starting to figure out who I was.' But dark, opiate clouds were lowering over the elegant Parisian skyline. The city was shrouded in heroin, the drug gaining a bleak ascendancy over softer, relatively anodyne medications and, of course, the music:

> I woke up one day, and instead of thinking about finding a band, I was thinking about if I was going to score... Every day, it became more apparent that I wasn't going to find what I was looking for in Paris. What good was Paradise to me now? What was the point of the Garden of Eden with no Adam and no apple?

Hungry for perpetual change, Chrissie returned to Akron. Not to parental refuge – as if that wouldn't have been stifling enough – but to a 'self-imposed high-security prison: no money, no job, no setup, no idea and, the most scary part, no hash'. The ennui was eased thanks to a brief stint depping for the hospitalised lead singer with a veteran Cleveland R&B outfit called The Mr Stress Blues Band. Thanks to the future Golden Palominos drummer Anton Fier, Chrissie landed a singing job with Jack Rabbit, a Cleveland group formed by an old friend, Duane Vehr, and a Floridian guitar hero, Donnie Baker. Now with a regular gig, the hash famine resolved by a timely first-aid parcel from Sasha in Paris, Chrissie felt settled enough to decline an invitation from McLaren to return to London, on his dime, to be in on the genesis of a new band called The Love Boys.

By the mid-1970s, Cleveland was in post-industrial decline. Battered by Lake Erie tornadoes and dubious insurance fires, the city was virtually ruled by the Mafia and mired in one of America's highest murder rates. After Jack Rabbit flopped, Chrissie answered an ad to tend bar at the Garfield Hotel: 'a number-runners' joint with the regulars starting on bourbon at eight in the morning'. The gig's main requirement seemed to be a working knowledge of firearms; a loaded handgun sat permanently in a drawer within easy reach of both the bartender and whichever wiseguy might be in the room disputing his bill. Chrissie accepted the position, only to be sacked after a week for scoring dope from a customer.

During a brief break in Arizona, she received a telegrammed invitation from a bassist named Michael Fradji Memmi to join his band in Paris. Memmi was an addled biker veteran of the 1968 Sorbonne student riots. His group, the Frenchies, for whom Chrissie first sang lead at L'Olympia supporting the

Flamin' Groovies, was another that preferred operatic drug consumption to coherent music. After an aborted meeting at the Féte Rouge festival with Nick Lowe – she'd known the songwriter, multi-instrumentalist and producer since her days with *NME* and his with pub-rockers Brinsley Schwarz – Chrissie befriended the guitarist Chris Spedding, who was then playing with John Cale's band.

Returning to England in 1976, Chrissie's networking slowly bore fruit. Through McLaren she met another aspiring manager, Bernie Rhodes, and guitarist Mick Jones. Quickly bonding, Hynde and Jones began to write songs. Perhaps it was only the arrival of the charismatic Joe Strummer, and Rhodes' preference for an all-male lineup, that frustrated the chances of an equally compelling American female singer fronting The Clash, one of the finest bands of the period. When Mick invited her to join as a non-performer on their first UK tour, Chrissie's disillusionment grew. She told *Rolling Stone*:

> It was great, but my heart was breaking. I wanted to be in a band so bad. And to go to all the gigs, to see it so close up, to be living in it and not to have a band, was devastating to me. When I left, I said, 'Thanks a lot for lettin' me come along', and I went back weeping on the underground throughout London. All the people I knew in town were all in bands. And there I was, like the real loser, you know?

'Chrissie seemed to be falling by the wayside', The Damned's bassist, Captain Sensible, told deejay Johnnie Walker in 2014. 'She waited long enough to play the guitar because she didn't want to be a clichéd woman in rock. [Women] were treated pretty appallingly back in the seventies.' But it was the salad days of UK punk, and expectations were under new management. Opportunities, good and bad, came and went like whack-a-mole. As The Sex Pistols began scaring the bejazus out of a somnolent middle Britain, Chrissie hooked up once more with one of the band's frontbenchers, guitarist Steve Jones.

The punk movement was about to gain the notoriety McLaren craved. Early in 1977, the Pistols' talented bassist Glen Matlock was ill-advisedly ousted in favour of a friend from John Lydon's youth called John Simon Ritchie, who hung around SEX and whom Rotten had dubbed 'Sid Vicious' after his pet hamster. Sid stumbled into the Pistols' purview only to find the easiest of Matlock's basslines beyond him, although his creative wielding of a bike chain was beyond compare. The instability delighted the chaos-seeking McLaren, who saw in the newcomer's excesses only another perfect media storm. 'If Johnny Rotten is the voice of punk,' the Chelsea shopkeeper pronounced, 'then Vicious is the attitude.'

Beset with visa and cashflow problems, Chrissie's continuing UK tenure looked shaky. Desperate to avoid deportation to the US, she agreed to marry Sid: a nihilistic liability, certainly, but one that at least came with a British passport. Prospects of long-term connubial bliss as Mrs Vicious were dashed when the groom jilted his blushing bride for a magistrate, before whom Sid was compelled to answer for putting out someone's eye with a glass. Whether Chrissie demanded Sid refund her generous dowry of two pounds is not known. (For the record it should be stated that, unlike most of polite society, Chrissie held the errant Pistol in some regard: 'Sid was very sweet and very honest,' she told the *Independent* in 2003. 'He really told you what he thought. He was so non-discriminating... it's a shame about Sid.')

A more promising marriage, almost as short-lived, was with another McLaren brainwave called Masters Of The Backside. Chrissie's lead vocals/guitar would be supported by her briefly-redeemed ex, Nick Kent, on guitar, drummer Chris Miller, bassist Ray Burns and singer/guitarist David Zero. The group quickly called time, scared away by McLaren's obsessive control freakery and the swiftly resumed Hynde-Kent standoff. Miller, however, had spotted Chrissie's potential to become more figurehead than galley slave: 'So outrageous,' he told Pretenders biographer Chris Salewicz. 'She was the first punk bird.' (Miller, Burns and Zero would reinvent themselves respectively as Rat Scabies, Captain Sensible and Dave Vanian, adding guitarist Brian Robertson, aka Brian James, to form BritPunk's first and finest, The Damned.)

Chrissie continued to bounce from one 'small-time money-making scheme' to another. She designed T-shirts with artist and punk-somebody Judy Nylon; modelled for 75p an hour at St Martin's Art College; hung around with Terence Conran's biker son Sebastian; moved into a house with photographer and DJ Don Letts (where, in a room in which a previous housemate had committed suicide, Chrissie penned 'Private Life'); and connected again with Captain Sensible when another near-miss, The Unusuals, failed to get past rehearsals. The band, minus Chrissie, later reimagined themselves as sonic terrorists Johnny Moped.

In a world of whims and wideboys, with McLaren, Rhodes and Stiff Records' Jake Riviera already on speed-dial, Chrissie next met Tony Secunda, a veteran Mr Ten Percent and a grizzled survivor of the 1960s rock business. Secunda had brought success to artists as diverse as Tyrannosaurus Rex, The Moody Blues, Procol Harum and The Move. However, he'd missed out on punk, a genre that ran on similar shock tactics to those he'd pioneered a decade or more before. Chrissie remarked in *Reckless*:

> Everything that went before got thrown onto the rubbish heap with no respect or apologies. When someone told Tony about an American girl with a guitar and an attitude who'd been skulking around the scene for some time to no avail, he must have thought it might be his way back in.

Secunda invited Chrissie to his office to hear her tear off the chords – without lyrics – to an insistent, oddly-metred but undeniably rocking thrash called 'The Phone Call'. Perhaps it was her manner – the American girl with the attitude 'stared him down with a defiant glare' – but the smitten magnate began parading Chrissie around town as his latest wunderkind. She signed nothing, caring little for a solo career, wanting 'to be *in* a band, not singled-out'. She was happy to bide her time and hang with Tony. Needing a demo disc, she invited bassist Mal Hart, Motörhead's drummer Phil Taylor and an engineer to a small Denmark Street studio to record a few of her songs. She emerged with 'The Phone Call' and 'Hymn No. 4'. An alternative account of this session places Chrissie at an eight-track studio off the King's Road, teamed with Johnny Moped bassist Fred Mills and Nigel Pegrum, percussionist with another Secunda signing, Steeleye Span. Nigel's presence was less counter-intuitive than it looked, given his previous gig; prior to toughening up the previously drummer-free Span, he worked with such heavy hitters as early Uriah Heep and The Small Faces. When Steeleye split four months after the King's Road date, Chrissie asked Nigel to join the tyro Pretenders, an invitation he declined. Perhaps the drummer considered 17 years of non-stop wassailing enough. Later regretting the decision, Nigel's take on his temporary boss's compositional traits was incisive:

> She had a very strong idea of how her songs should sound. They relied very much on her feel for rhythm, as they'd all been written on the guitar … As soon as I sat down at the drums and tried to play a simple 4/4 beat, it all became very awkward. Her writing … was not within the conventions of time signatures, often because of the controlling influence of her lyrics. More often than not, she had to add another bar onto the end of a line simply because she'd decided to tag on another word.

In Mick Farren's memoir *Give The Anarchist A Cigarette* – Chrissie knew the writer, musician and agitpropper from her *NME* days, flat-shared with Mick's estranged wife Joy and provided backing vocals on his fine 1978 album *Vampires Stole My Lunch Money* – Mick commended the American's 'strange and compelling' songs:

> Her devil-may-care disregard for the accepted conventions of rhyme patterns and standard verse structures was stunning. Although they sounded nothing like her, the only people I could think of who worked in this way were Syd Barrett, [Tyrannosaurus Rex's Steve] Took and, now and then, Neil Young.

Chrissie's next misadventure was with The Moors Murderers, a trashy mishmash comprising SEX alumnus Steve Strange, bassist Mal Hart, Sid Vicious' flatmate Soo Catwoman and future Clash drummer Topper Headon. Seeking a guitarist, Strange asked Chrissie (who knew little of the 1960s Yorkshire atrocities which the future Visage singer thought would supply such a cool name) to play in an industry showcase. During the performance, Strange used aliases to introduce the band, whose faces were obscured by

KKK-like bin-liners. For the benefit of the press, if not the publicity-hungry Strange, Chrissie was dubbed 'Christine Hyndley'. Unsurprisingly the infantile punning soon fetched up at the *NME*, which was pleased to report a gig by its former staffer 'Chrissie Hynd' and 'her' band, The Moors Murderers. Worse still, the tabloids seized on the story as yet another example of how punk was eating children and barfing the undigested results over the moral majority. Secunda was appalled, possibly because Strange, not he, had dreamed up the whole grisly idea. The ensuing gripes shed enough bad blood permanently to alienate Chrissie and her budding manager. At which point emerged an industry insider named Greg Shaw, who, in return for an evening of basic guitar tuition, brokered another useful introduction. Dave Hill, an A&R with Anchor Records, was putting together a list of artists for his own venture, Real Records. Hill was impressed, as Chrissie later told *Melody Maker*:

> Dave just got more and more keen. I said, look, I've got a rehearsal place, but I'm about £70 in arrears, and basically, I've got fuck all, man, I haven't got a band or anything. So I expected him to say, well, come around when you've got something together, but he didn't. He said, I'll pay off the debt you've got here ... and we'll just advertise for musicians and I'll leave you to it and I'll just aid you. As he got more involved, he decided to leave having the record label and just manage us.

Briefly there was talk of Chrissie joining the Stranglers. This felt logical following the Murderers, but any liaison with the wilfully macho Guildford band would surely have burned enough post-feminist propellant to torch Covent Garden. Seeing no room in his group for a third singer, guitarist Hugh Cornwell spiked the idea, hinting at how things might have gone by dubbing her 'Chrissie Hyndeleg'. Meanwhile Chrissie made friends with another Secunda client, Motörhead's larger-than-life bassist Lemmy Kilmister: the prototypical rock 'n' roll beast, for whom sex, drugs, Jack Daniels, motorcycles, Nazi daggers and beyond-the-wire excess were just another day at the office. Lemmy would later be instrumental in realising Chrissie's dream of forming a band, as she told *Rolling Stone* in 2020:

> He was like the quintessential example of everything, to me, that epitomises the rock experience. The way he thought, the way he looked ... the way he always had goofy-looking chicks standing next to him. Without Lemmy, I wouldn't have The Pretenders.

Chrissie sofa-surfed around Lemmy's Ladbroke Grove manor: west London's own Haight-Ashbury, a shabby relic of unmodernised Victoriana and floundered urban-renewal schemes. Among Lemmy's circle of bikers, Rastas and speed freaks was a percussionist from Hereford, in the west of England, who improbably styled himself Gas Wild. Thanks to Lemmy, the group

Chrissie had long sought would finally enjoy the services of a drummer – for about five minutes, anyway.

By spring 1978, Peter Granville Farndon (born 12 June 1952) was recovering from druggy diversions in Hong Kong and 'watching his teeth rot'. Until 1976, the alumnus (expelled) of Hereford Cathedral School had played with Cold River Lady, spent two years in Sydney with Aussie folk-rockers The Bushwackers and then returned to his home city. Following fisticuffs with the esteemed bassist Jet Harris (apparently for ogling the ex-Shadow's girlfriend), Pete received word from his pal Gas in London: this pushy American girl who sings, plays guitar and writes songs wants to form a band. Are you interested? It sounded good. Pete, teeth straightened, arranged to meet Gas and Chrissie in a Portobello Road bar. As he told *Rolling Stone*:

> I walked into the pub and there was this American with a big mouth across the other side of the bar. She said hi and turned around and ignored me for about an hour … Am I gonna be in a band with this cunt?

If this was a classic case of feigned indifference, it seemed to work, for within a month of their meeting the pushy American girl and the bassist would be romancing. The next stop was a rehearsals basement, and lively takes on King Floyd's 'Groove Me' and three Hynde originals: a country-&-western spoof she'd written on the road to Tucson called 'Tequila', 'Precious' and 'The Phone Call', which Pete identified as 'the heaviest fucking punk-rocker you could do in 5/4 time … I was very impressed.'

Two fellow Herefordians, guitarist James Honeyman-Scott (born 4 November 1956) and drummer Martin Dale Chambers (born 12 September 1951), had been playing in a group called Cheeks with Mott the Hoople's former organist, Verden Allen. James then gigged with a nondescript hard-rock band, its name lost to history. Following a stint with a prog-rock three-piece called Karakorum, Martin headed to London to hustle drumming sessions around a day job as a driving instructor. As Jimmy Scott tended his Hereford vegetable patch and worked in a music store, Pete phoned to suggest an audition for the new group. There followed one of the most fortuitous set-ups in rock history.

Gas Wild had a habit of getting too loaded to stay upright on his drum stool. This alone was probably no dealbreaker, but once personal overindulgences were allowed to affect the group and their music, it was likely game over – as Hynde would bitterly discover. This *was* rock 'n' roll, though; if Chrissie really wanted a motorcycle club with guitars, abstinence was unlikely to be part of the job description. A better fit might have been Lemmy's drummer, Phil Taylor. A former jazz percussionist, Taylor seemed an odd fit for Motörhead, who were essentially a punk-metal tactical assault team. His later sub-Keith Moon tendencies, however, would inspire the moniker 'Phil(thy Animal)'. Chrissie quietly hoped Phil might be lured away from Lemmy, but given the still more terrifying reputation of Phil's boss, this was a high-risk strategy, as she wrote:

> I wanted Taylor for myself, but that was something I would never have said out loud ... he was the property of Lemmy. I would never dream of poaching anyone from another band even if I could, but word on the street was that [Johnny Thunders'] Heartbreakers had their sights on Taylor. There were always rumours that Motörhead might be spitting up.

Chrissie's ruse could have been fabricated by the master puppeteer himself, Malcolm McLaren. Reasoning that if Thunders really was circling with intent to peck at a desiccated Motörhead, she could tactfully give Phil a taste of her budding group and let him make up his own mind. With her drum chair apparently a poisoned chalice, she asked Taylor to help audition a guitarist: '[Phil] would only be stepping in to help out and inadvertently getting a lug-hole of our repartee.' All she required was a proficient, pliable axeman who could either be dropped or kept, depending on what happened next.

Since Motörhead were definitely staying together, the Taylor stratagem was thankfully shelved. Nonetheless Jimmy arrived in London four months after Pete to meet Chrissie and her anointed bassist. The initial antipathy between Hynde and Honeyman-Scott was ominous: 'He probably thought I was just some loudmouth and I thought he was too smooth a player', Chrissie wrote, citing the guitarist's dismissal of punk for its lack of musicality and his (contextually) irksome admiration for The Beach Boys and ABBA. Jimmy himself was at first uncertain: having already acquired a taste for amphetamines, he told *Rolling Stone*, 'They had to pay me in money and drugs to come down and work with them.' At first he thought the band too loud; 'but as soon as I cranked some powders up me nose, I became interested.' Jimmy's stoked levity disguised the fact that something special was happening, as everyone discovered during a Regent Sounds Studio session booked by Hill. Chrissie recounted:

> I sat down to listen to the demos. I was stunned. I listened again; the songs had taken on another life. These weren't my songs anymore – they were ours ... Jimmy would transform my songs in a way I could only have hoped for in my wildest imaginings.

Drummer Gas Wild was replaced briefly by future hypnotherapist Jon Adkin, then by a jobbing thumper who also worked with London R&B band Juice On The Loose, Gerry Mcilduff. The session realised six songs, among them 'Precious', 'I Can't Control Myself', a song Chrissie had written about Pete's habit of hanging around pinball arcades called 'The Wait' and, most significantly for Chrissie and her new associates' immediate future, Ray

Davies' 'Stop Your Sobbing'. Chrissie ensnared her guitar prospect with the opportunity to work with her friend Nick Lowe; Jimmy was an admirer, both of the talented musician as a solo and of Lowe's work with Brinsley Schwarz and the Welsh guitar maven, Dave Edmunds. Nick was left cold by much of the demo, which Chrissie had hustled like crazy merely to get heard. Though he was unconvinced by the band's arrangement of the old Kinks song, Nick loved Chrissie's delivery, as he told Chris Salewicz (displaying undisguised disdain for two of the most celebrated female rockers in history): 'Her voice was fantastic. It was totally different from what she'd been using before, which was that Janis Joplin-stroke-Maggie Bell squawk that I find grossly offensive yet which so many girl singers seem to choose.' He agreed to produce a first single, coupling 'Stop Your Sobbing' with 'The Wait', at his Eden Studio in Chiswick.

Chrissie, Jimmy, Pete and Gerry worked up a set. On 26 August 1978, Dave Hill secured a maiden gig supporting fellow Real signings The Strangeways at Unity Hall in Wakefield, Yorkshire, the new quartet labouring under the Lowe-concocted name of Dinosaurs Eating Cars. The date was followed two months later by a week's residency at the Gibus Club in Paris and a Beatlesque, dues-paying tour around France. As Chrissie put it:

> The music was coming alive, but there was one thing that didn't sit right. Gerry was a competent drummer, but he was working in another band on the side … I wasn't at all happy if anyone had an agenda that took precedence over the band … he got the job done, but musically, something just didn't fit.

Although Chrissie, Jimmy and Pete hung out together, the older musician seemed semi-detached. His loyalties were divided between his bandmates and three kids from a failed marriage in Northern Ireland, to whom he regularly sent money. With Gerry proving no more feasible in the long term than Gas Wild, the band caught the attention of a genuine music-biz bigwig. Brooklyn-born Seymour Stein, tough-talking and old-school, had helped develop The Ramones and Talking Heads, rechristened punk as the less-confrontational 'new wave' and would soon be cutting discs for a promising young singer out of Bay City, Michigan called Madonna Ciccone. Keen to concentrate on managing Chrissie's band, Hill sold his youthful record company to Stein's label, Sire (although Real Records remained a brand badge for the first few Pretenders releases).

Everything short of unsolved gardening accidents was continuing to siphon off potential drummers. Mcilduff followed Wild to the dumpster (Gerry was personally dismissed by Chrissie, who eased his pain with £200 and a chunk of resin) and with closure now urgent, Pete and Jimmy belatedly thought of Martin Chambers. Their fellow Herefordian, now living in nearby Tufnell Park, needed no second invitation. His beefy, exuberant hammering and

Ringo-like rhythmic dependability proved perfect for the embryonic group. His flair for changes had been honed by prog dabblings with Karakorum, and his stint with a fourteen-piece, Glenn Miller-style dance orchestra led by Dave Stewart (not that one, or even the other one). 'As soon as I heard Martin thumping away on 'Precious', I started laughing so hard I had to turn my face to the wall', Chrissie recounted. 'When I recovered my composure, I turned to face the band I'd been searching for.' Martin agreed, telling Valerie Simadis:

> I don't know whether I used my kit or Gerry's kit, but I was a bit apprehensive about that. I went into this little dungeon of a room, and it's been well documented that Chrissie turned to the wall and started laughing to herself because it all worked ... Pete was the same, and when we first played these awkward timing songs, we did something like 'The Phone Call', and bang! It was just 90% there.

The band still hadn't a name. They briefly considered the Rhythm Method, then decided it was too risqué (this in the era of The Dead Kennedys, The Nipple Erectors, Throbbing Gristle and The Moors Murderers). Soon the first two sides were pressed, the single's sleeves and labels poised for the printer, Hill's publicity machine oiled and ready. As the office clamoured for branded product, Chrissie remembered an ex-boyfriend, a sergeant-at-arms with a south London biker gang, blushingly confessing his favourite song. It was a guilty secret he preferred not to share with his sterner colleagues. Chrissie finally decided her band's name would be based on Sam Cooke's version of a 1955 Platters song: 'The Great Pretender'.

The Pretenders would make their most valuable donations to popular culture before 1990. In 1986, Chrissie Hynde began her ascent to the benign dictatorship she never wanted, a situation even her powerful personality might have sidestepped had the motorcycle gang with guitars not been kettled by tragedy. (Jimmy Scott's vision for The Pretenders was probably the equal of Chrissie's; as a musical director, who knows where time and moderation might have taken him had heroin not taken him first?)

From then till now, Chrissie has been attended by carefully chosen friends, associates and session musicians. Her own 'way of doing things' has proven pliable, reflecting a broader shift in the composition of the prototypical rock-group. For rock's traditional nuclear family has atomised. Many major groups have shrunk their personnel to a few VIPs and an ever-changing pool of lessers. And a new guitarist 15 years into a successful band's reign rarely enjoys their predecessor's popularity or recognition, still less those of their employers. (Some of us are still coming to terms with Ronnie Wood, and before him Mick Taylor, replacing Brian Jones in The Rolling Stones. And remind me again, who's been The Stones' regular bass player since the departure of Bill Wyman? Thought not.)

So this history is curtailed by design in 1990 with The Pretenders' fifth album, *Packed!*, objectively a fine pop-rock record, but somehow lacking in the vim, vigour, shit and sugar of the first three. Despite an occasional lapse into conservative, by-the-numbers product rather than unlikely time signatures, semi-madcap inspiration and dirty rebel glee, subsequent records have shown that Chrissie's ear for a great tune and an incisive lyric has not dulled, even if the years have taken their toll. It's a good trick if you can do it: few rock artists approach their golden jubilee with music as vital and youth-affirming as at its birth. 2023's *Relentless*, The Pretenders' most recent release at the time of writing, is a good, solid, state-of-the-art rock 'n' roll album, with fine songs, a powerful crunch and even a lineup that's been relatively stable since 2008, if mainly for touring. But *Pretenders* it ain't.

It took a gale-force personality to steady the buffs after the hideous disfigurement of the early 1980s. With the losses of immy and Pete, The Pretenders in their purest form ended. Never again would this be a band of siblings; rightly or wrongly, 'Chrissie Hynde' and 'The Pretenders' remain one and the same. Chrissie is founder, head of state, CEO, HR consultant, PR guru, mentor, inspiration, spirit guide, Chief Poobah... *Leader*. The band's songs are, with a few exceptions, *her* songs, not a dollar bill between the individual and the collective. Wanna know the reasons for The Pretenders' enduring appeal? There you go.

Pretenders (1980)

Personnel
Chrissie Hynde: guitars, vocals
James Honeyman-Scott: guitars, keyboards, vocals
Pete Farndon: bass, vocals
Martin Chambers: drums, vocals
Produced at Wessex Studios, London; Air Studios, London, by Chris Thomas, Nick Lowe
Engineers: Bill Price, Steve Nye, Mike Stavrou
Released: January 1980
Highest chart position: UK: 1, US: 10

> We were all a little in love with Chrissie because she was so cool and didn't take any shit from anybody. She had so much style. She had a tough but vulnerable sound that was really unusual.
> Nick Lowe, sleeve notes for 2006 Pretenders compilation, *Pirate Radio*

> This is one of the most astonishing debut albums in the history of music.
> Michael Chabon

Pretenders is, indeed, one of rock's defining debuts. Nearly five decades after its release, its opening salvo remains the group's paradigm, a tantalising taste of where its A-Team might have travelled in the longer term had the guitarist and bass player not danced so intimately with Mr D.

A sizzling crucible of punky snarl, Stonesy swagger and Kinksy pop, *Pretenders* kicks away like a Bonneville hitting the ton on the North Circular, rages through a frantic first side, recovers its composure with a parcel of roguishly streetwise, near-perfect pop songs and crashes home almost 50 minutes later with a bass-driven stormer that manages to fuse Stevie Wonder with The Spencer Davis Group and Magazine. At a time when UK punk was morphing into post-punk, thereafter to the new romantics and synthpop, *Pretenders* evidenced seamless shifts in style and tone that briskly distanced its makers from every other contemporary rock 'n' roll band or genre.

Three hit singles were tucked up nicely by the time the album was released in January 1980. Each was more successful than the last, climaxing with a global monster. Onstage, the band were now combustible; confidence was high for the maiden long-player, even as the energy generated live was becalmed by the gentler pop sensibilities of the singles. All would be included on the album, contrasting intriguingly with the switchblade rock 'n' roll at which the young band were proving themselves as keen and bright as any of their peers.

The first 45, 'Stop Your Sobbing', coupled with 'The Wait', had been issued almost exactly a year before the album, charting in the UK at number 34. At around the same time, the band played their first bill-topping gig, at West Hampstead's Moonlight Club. As they proceeded to tear up live venues throughout the UK, critics were suitably ecstatic. Having already featured the band on *Melody Maker*'s coveted front page, editor Richard Williams attended a Moonlight set and, in his praise, evoked maybe the greatest of all rama-lama rock groups: 'The Wait' [is] the best thing of its kind I've heard since The MC5's 'Looking At You'... Chrissie Hynde deals with rock 'n' roll like no woman I've ever seen.' Over at *NME*, Nick Kent at first skewered the rival title's eagerness ('Five gigs played and the vultures are already congregating'), but Chrissie's ex was ultimately magnanimous ('As a dance band, there's simply no-one to touch them right now'). The critical hyperbole meant overall expectations for *Pretenders* had become lip-smackingly Beatles-esque, although as the band headed for the studio, one professional who could boast real-world Fabs experience was only a second choice.

For production duties, Chrissie at first fancied her old drinking partner, Nick Lowe, who by 1978 was a much sought-after writer, performer and producer. However 'Basher' (the nickname referenced Nick's mantric encouragement to his clients: 'bash it out, we'll tart it up later') was dubious about the music. He considered 'Stop Your Sobbing' the only early Pretenders demo with any real promise, limiting his contribution accordingly. It was a decision he'd regret, as he confessed to Chris Salewicz:

> I honestly didn't think the group were going to be as good as it turned out to be. I was really madly off the rama-lama punk thing at the time, and I thought that was the way Chrissie was going to go – which was really unfair because I'd never seen them or heard any of the other stuff she'd been writing. In fact, I didn't realise Chrissie could write such good songs. And I turned them down...

For the bulk of the album, Chrissie – if she was avowedly not a solo artist, she was just as certainly the gangmaster and main decisionmaker – enticed Chris Thomas with a demo cassette and a performance at the Marquee. She'd met the experienced producer in 1977, first at a Stranglers gig, later when Thomas helmed Chris Spedding's *Hurt*, the first record ever to feature Hynde's voice, albeit as backing vocalist. (Chrissie's knowledge of the Heavy Bikers might also have helped Spedding's lyrics; the versatile guitarist's resumé ran from free jazz to the Wombles, but his 1975 hit 'Motorbikin' suggested that behind the absent time signatures and the furry burrowers' ever-present litter bins lurked a down-the-line rocker.) Thomas – whose studio and personal skills had enhanced records by the heads of state themselves, The Beatles, along with such courtiers as Pink Floyd, The Sex Pistols, Procol Harum and Roxy Music – agreed to help largely on the evidence of 'Brass In Pocket', which he thought was the perfect single: 'I knew Chrissie was great and I really liked her songs,' Thomas told Salewicz. 'So what she suggested was that we do some really casual recording without worrying about what the consequences of it would be.'

Thomas was in demand. The Wessex Studios sessions for *Pretenders* had to be scheduled in numerous discrete quanta around the producer's obligations to Pete Townshend's *Empty Glass* and Wings' *Back To The Egg*. Perversely, this stumbling modus operandum did The Pretenders' recorded results no harm, allowing the band the space between studio sessions to evolve and refine the material around the UK club scene. As Thomas told *Uncut* in 2013:

> We did it in short bursts over the course of eight months. It was frustrating for them, but it meant Chrissie kept coming in with a fresh supply of brilliant new songs, like 'Lovers Of Today'.

Those consequences, of course, would prove unforgettable. The perfect second 45, 'Kid', backed by 'Tattooed Love Boys', was released in June 1979, peaking at number 33 after *Record Mirror* declared it single of the week. But just as Thomas had predicted, it was the third 7", 'Brass In Pocket' c/w 'Space Invader', that made the biggest impression. Shortly before the album hit the stores the single made number one in the UK – fittingly for a band with such promise for the upcoming 1980s, the decade's near-firstchart topper (Pink Floyd's 'Another Brick In The Wall, Part II' actually straddled the 1979 Christmas/New Year season in the top spot) – and number 14 on the US *Billboard* Hot 100. One week after its release, *Pretenders* entered the UK album chart at number one.

Critical reception was strangely mixed, but The Pretenders were about to go global. Success hastily reversed the polarities; suddenly every ligger who snubbed the support act they'd never heard of back in 1978 now insisted they'd always thought The Pretenders the best band in the world. *Melody Maker* and *NME* continued their feud: the former praised *Pretenders* as 'the first important album of the 1980s', while the latter, now ambushed by its 'hip young gunslingers' Julie Burchill and Tony Parsons (themselves influenced by a younger but no less vitriolic Chrissie Hynde – *NME* was doing for rock journalism what Hunter S. Thompson once did for political reporting), moaned that its mortal enemy was overhyping a band who were 'so reminiscent of '60s pop that any claim they are innovative is completely invalid.' *Sounds*, meanwhile, bafflingly detected two main influences: Public Image Ltd and Sting. It's hard to imagine who found the idea more hilarious, The Pretenders included. A decade after its release, *Pretenders* was declared by *Rolling Stone* the 20th-best album of the 1980s, upgrading its assessment in 2013 to the 13th-best debut album of all time.

For the sleeve, photographer Chalkie Davies nailed the band in all their insubordinate and, according to Martin, inebriated glory. On the left, Pete is bad-boy biker incarnate in greased quiff and black Brando 'Triumph' jacket; he seems startled, as if collared after guzzling a cappuccino at the Ace Café and doing a runner. On the right, a tall, supercool Jimmy peers down through rock 'n' roll aviator shades, appraising Martin's cheery grin, scruffy estate agent's three-piece suit and half-mast tie. Chrissie, of course, is the focal point, ruddily incandescent against her colleagues' dark attire. Like Pete's, her biker jacket is Lewis Leathers, only in scarlet: it looks the business, but questionable given the vegetarianism she'd observed since she was 17 and for which, one day, she'd willingly step outside the law. Interestingly pale and kohl-eyed, she gazes with basilisk contempt through raven bangs, inspired, it's said, by Jane Asher; stonily impassive, oozing the dangerous sexuality she was steadily trademarking. Rarely has the essence of a rock 'n' roll band – and a rock 'n' roll bandleader – been so exquisitely captured.

'Precious' 3.38 (Chrissie Hynde)
First album, first track, first lyrical dropping of the F-bomb, first of numerous putdowns of people Chrissie felt had not been especially helpful to her yet youthful career. 'Precious' sets out The Pretenders' stall in no uncertain terms, Martin's sticks counting in an urgent, punky gallop for the singer to issue a torrent of whip-smart one-liners. She evokes her earlier years and formative *liaisons dangereuses* around East 55th/Euclid Avenue and the Sterling Hotel, a notorious 1970s haunt of Cleveland crooks and call girls. At the line, 'But you know I was shittin' bricks 'cause I'm precious', Jimmy's phased and treated guitar slides greasily into the chorus, driven hard by a bass run from Pete that plunges like a hooker's neckline. At 2.17, Jimmy swoops in with a police siren, the whole shebang now sounding like a pay-night bar crawl around downtown Akron with the good ol' boys from Goodyear. Chrissie's rapping is clipped and pungent, making damn sure that anyone boarding this breathless new trip knows exactly what they're in for. If you've crossed the line, expect no mercy.

The first recipient on record of the wrath of Hynde is 'Mr Stress', *nom-de-musique* of Bill Miller, a harpist and bandleader of Cleveland renown. When Miller briefly employed a younger Chrissie, the venerable bluesman verbally doubted her commitment to the devil's music, tactfully hinting that only in Europe would anyone bother to listen to her. Now from that same region, she reminds the prophetic sourpuss of how it was she, not he, who escaped local herodom and parochial smothering in Ohio:

> Now Howard the Duck and Mr Stress both stayed
> Trapped in a world that they never made
> But not me baby I'm too precious I had to fuck off.

Hell of a way to conclude the opening statement. Not even The Sex Pistols had the balls.

'The Phone Call' 2.30 (Hynde)
If 'Precious' is vicious, 'The Phone Call' is downright malevolent. Its sinister words, once again more murmured than sung, imply conspiracy and intrigue, its paranoid message apparently delivered by one of the gangsters Chrissie used to serve at the Garfield Hotel:

This is a mercy mission
From a faceless messenger who don't wanna see you hit
Here's the word
Listen to it
Somebody that you used to know is back in town
You better go.

Chrissie has explained that, with a friend's ex-partner headed back to town bent on violent retribution, the only way to alert the threatened quarry is via an anonymous phone call. As recounted at length in *Reckless*, Chrissie's younger days were peppered with dalliances with the Heavy Bikers – most likely Hell's Angels – who plied their trade around Akron and Cleveland. Since these encounters had a habit of turning ugly, Chrissie's unwillingness to identify herself as she warns her friend suggests that, once the city limits have been breached by the vengeful squadron of soft-tail Harleys, she'll be just as imperilled.

Deemed by Pete Farndon to be 'the heaviest fucking punk-rocker you could do in 5/4 time', 'The Phone Call' is mainly in 7/4, a teasingly difficult measure rare in commercial pop records (Pink Floyd's 'Money' is one of the few) and more likely to be found on complex prog-rock epics. At 0.55, the stuttering metre of the opening bars hits the bridge with a conventional 4/4 and the use of the fabled tritone, or flatted fifth. More colourfully badged the Devil's Interval, the tritone was banned by the early Catholic church for its allegedly satanic properties. Centuries later, apostates from Camille Saint-Saëns to Jimi Hendrix and Black Sabbath were still summoning the tritone, while music lovers of greater piety cowered behind their crucifixes and stuck to safer fare. Lyrics aside, perhaps this explains 'The Phone Call's portentous flavour.

Retained from the original Denmark Street demo are the intro 'pips', phoned in by a certain avant-hero and name-to-drop, John Cale. For ages after, Tony Secunda proudly advised anyone who'd listen that his good buddy the former Velvet was now producing his protégé, Chrissie Hynde (Cale happened to be in the same room as Tony when the call was made). For later live performances of a song that was among Chrissie's favourites, Martin Chambers would usually be recalled for his mastery of the erratic changes. Devilish tritone included.

'Up The Neck' 4.28 (Hynde)

Chrissie's adventures at the Sterling Hotel and elsewhere in Cleveland's 'most depressed inner-city neighbourhood' were proving a fruitful source of songwriting inspiration. The third leg of *Pretenders*' opening 'Ohio' quartet, 'Up The Neck' recalls one harrowing night in 1975, and the comedown from a bout of acid-fuelled poontang with a stranger from whom Chrissie had inadvisedly blagged a ride. She described the events in *Reckless*, leaving little to the imagination; here some of her most abrasive lyrics act equally as lurid reportage, dismissive put-down and weird redemption, a portrait of a predatory, possibly dangerous libertine who nonetheless leaves his conquest feeling 'it was all rather run of the mill'.

Ambiguities abound. Chrissie concedes he could move 'with an animal skill' and she 'was sure his intentions were sweet', even if he *has* quietly dosed her with blue mescaline and hinted that things could get worse, perhaps even terminal. According to *Reckless*, she asks if he's ever been in love. In response, he despairingly laments someone who is 'dead, dead, dead', the non-sequitur a prelude to apparently sizing up Chrissie's neck for a nearby lamp cord. She escapes to the hall 'with my teeth in my head/up to my neck and I said said, said, said dead'.

So somewhere between lyrics written in 1978 and her 2016 memoir, Chrissie has transferred her acquaintance's potentially murderous disorientation to her own air of damaged resignation. In both book and song, the beauty-&-the-beast account of the sordid goings-on is oddly kind on the stranger: the sort of rascal Chrissie seemed drawn to as if to magnetic north. (Chrissie's apparent sexual subservience, which seems odd given her uncompromising outlaw persona, would prove a recurring trope in her songwriting.) Despite the violent sex and post-coital threat, we sense she finally gives him a pass. In the book, she records how he drove her home without problem, even returning two days later with the five bucks she'd loaned him. 'Baby, oh sweetheart', she croons at the end, a repeat of the key line from what passes as a chorus in another unusually structured song. The guitars toggle between McGuinn-style twinkling and two-note, Reed-style hammering, while the middle solo is intricate and repetitive. "Up The Neck' started off as a reggae song', Jimmy told music writer Jas Obrecht. 'I said, 'Let's speed it up', and put in that little guitar run.'

'Tattooed Love Boys' 2.59 (Hynde)
The album's fourth 'Ohio' movement chronicles another fragment of Chrissie Hynde's past, an incident again perhaps more serious than her colourful, slightly glib accounts suggest. One evening while off her face on quaaludes, she was gang-raped by the Heavy Bikers, whom she'd met briefly when the crew were hired as 'security' at a Paul Butterfield gig. After that first encounter at the gang's Nazi insignia-bedecked clubroom, Chrissie escaped unscathed – even these unangelic Angels drew the line at jailbait – but at 21, she was considered fair game. In another ambiguous passage from *Reckless*, adjusted with some hindsight, she seemed to blame her own doped-out naivité instead of assigning accountability to where it properly lay. The mistargeted *mea culpa* was most explicitly set out in the song:

> I was a good time, yeah, I got pretty good
> At changing tyres, upstairs bro'
> I shot my mouth off
> And you showed me what that hole was for.

In mitigation that must have had women's libbers printing up wanted posters, she later pleaded: 'However you want to look at it, this was all my doing and I take full responsibility. You can't fuck around with people who wear 'I heart rape' and 'On Your Knees' badges.'

Hmm. It's a bit like blaming sexual assault on a short skirt, a revealing neckline and overdone makeup, painting the woman not as a victim but as a wanton Jezebel who's obviously asking for it. This is, of course, clichéd misogynist bollocks and entirely unworthy of Chrissie Hynde. By trying too hard to avoid accusations of pamphleteering (her position on women's rights would prove inconsistent, as we shall see later), she not only delivers the thugs to the moral high ground but makes them a welcoming cup of tea.

But if the sentiments are unconvincing (if elegantly put), the track is a killer: a sweaty, punky sugar-rush in rare-as-hens'-teeth 7/16 time, its Bo Diddley maracas rattling like a playschool while Chrissie, Pete and Martin shovel premium-grade bitumen into a fiercely locomotive rhythm. Jimmy answers with a chimingly tricky three-note progression and, at 1.39, a solo that slashes and shimmers equally. In 2018, producer Thomas told Bill Kopp how the stunning immediacy of 'Tattooed Love Boys' and 'Precious' was achieved:

> [They] were both rough mixes I did at the end of the night. And then, like two months later, I thought, well, I'm not going to mix those again – they sound perfect.

'Tattooed Love Boys' echoes the compositional pattern of numerous early Pretenders songs. Having written the bare bones, Chrissie fleshed them out with her bandmates, the outcome as much a consequence of instinct and feel as technique and songwriting prowess. Suck-it-and-see signatures and false climaxes were common, while Chrissie developed an almost telekinetic bond with Martin Chambers, the once and future king of The Pretenders' percussion throne despite furlough between 1986 and 1994. In 1980, Martin advised *Sounds*:

> I can understand her way of doing it. Take 'Tattooed Love Boys', where there's a gap. Normally, you'd count the beat through the silence so you can all come back in together. But not with Chrissie. No count, no way. It lasts as long as she wants it to last.

'Space Invader' 3.27 (Pete Farndon/James Honeyman-Scott)
A mechanised stegosaurus lumbers onto the forecourt of a peri-urban delicatessen. The deli owner, unwisely having crossed the local Mob, can only gape helplessly as the MAC sani-cruiser's driver ejects his entire putrid cargo of domestic waste across the drive and up to the front door. Thus begins Episode 11, Season 2 of the magisterial HBO gangland series *The*

Sopranos, all to the throbbing power-play of *Pretenders*' only all-instrumental track.

'Space Invader', which was also grabbed for an episode of *Miami Vice*, feels slight, a space marker amid the unfailing excellence of the songwriting encasing it. Nonetheless the tune has an interesting structure and an insistent drive, opening with Martin's big, roiling dollops of tom-tom and Pete's powerful bass riff, before Jimmy's assertive chording leads to a theme not a million miles from Lennon/McCartney's 'Day Tripper'. The band bash through to 1.48, the weightiness increasing before a brief return to the Beatley grist allows some respite. But by 2.50 it's remorseless, as if Jimmy, Pete and Martin are evoking not an innocent arcade diversion but, well, a rubbish truck tipping several foul-smelling tonnes of trash outside a caff (although the tune is used again later in *The Sopranos*, this time for the stoned afterglow of a love scene). At the end, the titular video game – hugely popular in 1979 – creeps in as a sample.

'The Wait' 3.37 (Hynde/Farndon)
Pete Farndon hadn't quite shaken his weakness for game arcades by the time he met Chrissie Hynde. Repeatedly waiting on Pete to finish lasering insurgent aliens inspired The Pretenders' chief to pen this great song. Yet 'The Wait' is not about the bassist per se; the words broaden beyond the observation of an innocently laddish activity to something darker, as if the gamer were among the feral young unfortunates who haunt gaming arcades only because they've nowhere else to go. Over another erratic metre, Chrissie's hiccupped words flood in like a stream of consciousness at spring tide, the song's lost boy coming home in the middle:

> I said child, child stare into the street light
> Messed up child, lonely boy tonight
> Kick the wall, turn the street and back again
> Oh boy you've been forgotten.

If 'Stop Your Sobbing' was near-perfect pop pastiche, it was far from representative of the ferocity of which the group were capable. But ahead of the album's release, no-one hearing the first single's B-side could doubt it: this was one lollapalooza of a rock 'n' roll band. Originally taped by Nick Lowe at Eden as the B-side of 'Stop Your Sobbing', now re-recorded by Thomas, 'The Wait' is satisfyingly frantic, Pete running up and down his bass like a sprinter at interval training. An exhilarating key change at 2.34, midway through a twinkling solo from Jimmy, was Farndon's idea. Had heroin not had its evil way, such initiative might have seen the bassist comfortably through to his old age; despite Scottie's counsel never to give her work away, Chrissie allowed herself to be talked by her then-lover Pete into handing over half the song's royalties.

'Stop Your Sobbing' 2.39 (Ray Davies)
In 1964, The Kinks' first album was rush-released to exploit the huge success of Ray Davies' game-changing 'You Really Got Me'. That masterly slab of proto-metal ('it wasn't called heavy metal when I invented it,' deadpanned Kinks guitarist and Ray's kid brother, Dave) blasted away from its adjacent material like a starship escaping a planet of bewildered primitives, such was its impact set against the workaday, if energetically punkish, covers and yet-unfledged Ray Davies originals.

Of the rest of *The Kinks*, however, another track felt equally out of place, though not in such a good way. Among the whiskery old R&B standards and some paper-thin ready-mades courtesy of producer Shel Talmy, all delivered by Ray in the adenoidal sneer that helped birth a thousand US garage bands, 'Stop Your Sobbing' was the deepest of deep cuts: a vaguely countrified, lachrymose plea to an ex-partner not to fret about being jilted.

The ex was likely not Rasa Didzpetris, a Lithuanian-born singer from Bradford, who provided backing vocals on *The Kinks* and whom Ray wedded that same year. As she oohs and aahs behind the chorus, the first Mrs Davies sounds oddly like the woman who was nearly the third. Given Chrissie would one day be engaged to Ray, one of her great rock 'n' roll heroes – even in her wildest teenage imaginings not something she could have foreseen in 1964 – this was uncanny indeed.

In the context of The Pretenders' own first album, 'Stop Your Sobbing' feels as incongruous as the original. This may be because it was the sole track desked by Nick Lowe, whose talents were among the bribes Chrissie used to ensnare Rockpile fan Jimmy Scott. Working on the recording at his Eden studio in Chiswick, Nick does a fine job on the one Pretenders' demo he thought hinted at any promise, reverbing and fattening out Davies' original until it sounds like it's bubbled up from a more Spectorish corner of the 1960s. It's easy to imagine a winsome lead vocal by the blessed Ronnie herself, cossetted by her flawed-genius husband in massed horns, percussion and voices.

But here the vocals are all Chrissie's, multitracked several times over Jimmy's jangling, ever-Byrdsy guitar and a solidly clumping rhythm laid down by Pete and Martin – a sort of Parapet of Sound, if you will. The singer's apparent duet with herself in the final bars was due to an unusually lengthy delay echo. Far from Chrissie singing the line 'Gotta stop sobbing, oh-oh' twice, a happy accident was triggered by Jimmy's cheeky tinkering with the desk, followed by Nick's own remedial response. To correct the timing, the producer used a machine that turned the spools only slowly. Recalls Lowe: 'It worked a treat. The song had real charm, and it was done so quickly.'

Backed by 'The Wait', 'Stop Your Sobbing' was released as a UK single in January 1979, charting at number 34. On 5 July 1980, the record made number 65 on the US Hot 100. More significantly for both writer and interpreter, by 1983 Chrissie would be cuddling Natalie, her and Ray's baby, and sailing – dangerously, given such a volatile pairing – close to marriage.

'Kid' 3.07 (Hynde)
When its progress through the UK singles chart stalled at number 33, 'Kid' was deemed a disappointment, especially after the promise of 'Stop Your Sobbing'. Four decades on, the song is rightly acclaimed as a melancholic masterclass in intelligent power-pop, a cherished regular on oldies' radio and cover bands' setlists.

As the first four tracks on (vinyl) side one of *Pretenders* demonstrate, Chrissie Hynde could stripe the UK's cultural jugular with all the gleefully savage efficiency of a Sid Vicious on speed. Side two arrives ringing with the minor-key Rickenbacker elegance of early-days Byrds and mid-period Beatles. Presaging the album's less frenetic half – until we reach the final track, that is – 'Kid' marks the point at which Hynde's original writing leaps to melodicism from harder-core punk and is the first song on the album fully to showcase the influence of unabashed pop fan Jimmy Scott. As Chrissie told Norwegian TV in 1990:

> [The Pretenders'] sound was very influenced by the people I was working with. [Jimmy] really brought the melody out in me. I was pretty punked out at the time. I had denied my melodic tendencies.

Jimmy advised Guitar Player in April 1981 of how Chrissie's early abrasiveness became tempered by his own gentler musicality, and how his input fed back into a virtuous loop as the singer responded positively:

> The melodic parts of the numbers really all started coming together by me putting in these little runs and licks. And then Chrissie started to like pop music, and that's why she started writing things like 'Kid'.

For once the songwriting is not autobiographical. 'It's about a prostitute whose son finds out what she does for a living,' Chrissie told the website UnmaskUs. 'This is her having a conversation with him.' The exchange between mother and son is poignantly understated, the composer displaying an admirable empathy with both parties. Chrissie delivers the lyrics with that slight, wavering vibrato she was rapidly trademarking; it's hard for the listener not to inhabit, as a partner with equivalent *simpatico*, the intimate domestic world she creates.

Prior to Chrissie clarifying the song's meaning, some fretted over whether the eponymous youth might be Pete Farndon, whose smack dependency was already chewing away at both his romance with Chrissie and the bassist's broader relationship with the band. Others wondered if 'Kid' addresses the vulnerabilities of Jimmy Scott, five years Chrissie's junior and whose *laissez-faire* take on the responsibilities of rock 'n' roll stardom masked a fragile, easily-bruised interior. If this is the case – and despite Chrissie's explanation, the lyrics are teasingly ambiguous enough – the guitarist rewards the writer's heartfelt concerns with a magnificent break at 1.30. Apparently Jimmy spent several days designing his solo ahead of recording. The result fits like a kid glove.

'Private Life' 6.27 (Hynde)
Elvis Costello nailed the effect of 'Private Life' with his usual pithiness: 'It's like every Joni Mitchell song rolled into one.' Since Chrissie's arrival in Europe – even before, given her colourful adolescence – the American had moved in circles where she tripped over 20 such people as the subject of 'Private Life' before breakfast. The song is another classically withering Hynde put-down, a verbal crucifix thrust before an unsuitable suitor who's not so much interestingly devilish as an unholy dullard. His identity is impossible to discern, but the would-be lover is likely a TV actor with a failed marriage and sexual hangups: regions of a private life in which the singer, understandably, does not wish to cohabit. She slays the wretched wannabe with every bitchy stanza:

> You asked me for advice I said use the door
> But you're still clinging to somebody you deplore
> And now you wanna use me for emotional blackmail
> I just feel pity when you lie, contempt when you cry.

A loping laziness about the music suits Chrissie's evidently bored mood. Far from spitting another razorbacked Hyndeian tirade, she wearily runs through the shopping list of reasons why she's distancing herself from her doomed courtier. The arrangement's comparative simplicity and lack of musical dynamics are cleverly at one with her disposition.

The music speaks to a certain July evening in 1975, when Bob Marley & The Wailers took London's Lyceum Theatre by force of arms. Reggae tore through the consciousness of white rock musicians like impis at Isandlwana, forcing players and critics alike into a radical re-evaluation of modern music. The arrangement of 'Private Life' tips The Pretenders' hat towards the seductive riddims of dub, with pattering rimshots, a massive running bassline, electronic colouring and plenty of reverb on Jimmy's glowingly insistent guitar. Later the same year, the disco diva Grace Jones would claim the song for Jamaica. The alleged virtues of her hit reading were lauded by Chrissie in the sleeve notes for Jones' 1998 Island anthology *Private Life: The Compass Point Sessions*:

> Like all the other London punks, I wanted to do reggae, and I wrote 'Private Life'. When I first heard Grace's version, I thought, 'Now that's how it's

supposed to sound!' In fact, it was one of the high points of my career – what with Sly and Robbie being the masters and Grace Jones with her scorching delivery. Someone told me it was [Island boss] Chris Blackwell's idea.

Hynde had a point, if only about La Jones' musical collaborators. By 1979, Sly Dunbar and Robbie Shakespeare had become the world's killer drums-bass affiliation, a two-bodies-one-mind tower of supernatural rhythmic telepathy. In their hands, and those of producers Blackwell and Alex Sadkin, Jones' 'Private Life' pops and shimmers, a slinky masterclass in modern dance. As for what's brought to the party by the flat-topped fashionplate herself, only an ex-model whose main claim to fame was bitch-slapping an English chat-show host on camera could exude such depths of sincerity, emotion and facial mobility.

'Brass In Pocket' 3.05 (Hynde/Honeyman-Scott)
From the opening bar of The Pretenders' third single and maiden UK number one (number 14 in the US), Chrissie and Jimmy brew up instant brand recognition, the band's signature chart statement strutting proudly alongside 'She Loves You', 'God Only Knows' and 'Waterloo Sunset' as examples of how to make a hit record for stellar perpetuity.

All the key elements – a catchy melody; perfect form and structure; smart, evocative lyrics; glistening production – are weaved into three assertively floor-filling minutes. In the context of the band's earliest trio of 45s, the song reminds the audience that its authors are a superlative hits machine, effortlessly radiating a pop awareness the equal of any. Within the album, meanwhile, 'Brass In Pocket' showcases the band's agility to morph from semi-housetrained punks to a sexy yet palatable foursome no *Top Of The Pops* producer could resist.

Although she's recognised its long-term service, for many years Chrissie professed to dislike 'Brass In Pocket', telling *American Songwriter* in 2020 it was 'trying to be a Motown song, but it didn't quite get it.' Was the Sound of Young America in her mind when she wrote it? The lyric, 'Been driving, Detroit leaning' – the latter a euphemistic pose, the driver lolling back in the seat, steering one-handed, left arm resting on the open sill – evokes both the Tamla Motown label's home city and the typically automobile-centric US rock 'n' roll music at which the band were proving themselves so adept. At such moments, it's worth remembering Chrissie Hynde's hinterland was not a million miles from the Motor City itself. Yet in spirit 'Brass In Pocket' carries two passports, straddling the Atlantic as readily as its composer. It may be as avowedly American in its heart as most pop music before or since, but the song's agency is Anglo-American in every way, with even a measure of rhyming slang thrown in to localise the knowing Americana.

In the promo video, a pink Cadillac – its driver, a too-cool-for-school Pete Farndon, affecting the nonchalant Detroit lean – incongruously rolls up outside a grimily beige and grimly English corner café and disgorges the band. Waiting in the restaurant, Chrissie's server has apparently been airlifted to the London eatery from a Midwest diner, recalling the singer's self-consciousness whenever cute guys clocked her waiting table during her studies at Kent State. Here she discovers that teasing her hair and making doe-eyes at Farndon won't dissuade the boys (soon to be draped in three likely lasses, despite Pete's sly eye contact with his then real-life paramour) from scurrying back to their wheels and leaving the singer to her dull routine. Chrissie might be confident that something special will happen with the gang's arrival, but she's quickly left high and dry, tearfully vulnerable as she watches the big, displaced vehicle and its partying occupants disappear into the North Kensington gloom. Chrissie wasn't mad about the tale's denouement, as she told Lindsey Parker of *Yahoo Music* in 2021:

> The video got hijacked by the director because the idea of that was that these guys were going to break in on motorcycles and I was going to get on the back and ride out of there. And he had different ideas, and he left me in there crying. That wasn't my script.

However, with the car and the café's oversized display pack of Lucky Strikes reinforcing the air of a dowdy, rainy provincialism briefly jolted into life by shots of exotica from across the pond – everyone looks a lot younger, cooler, feistier and more gorgeous than the usual patrons of English greasy spoons – the film actually meshes nicely with a song Chrissie titled after hearing an English northerner utter a chance remark about suits and dry cleaners. The lyric deals as much with the requisite arrogance of broader rock performance as it does the thwarted sexual anticipation so proficiently conveyed – unusually for an MTV promo – by the little comedy of manners that accompanies it:

> Got brass in pocket/Got bottle, I'm gonna use it
> Intention, I feel inventive
> Gonna make you, make you, make you notice.

Chrissie explained the song's meaning to *American Songwriter*:

> You're supposed to be kind of cocky and sure of yourself. You're not supposed to go on stage and say, 'I'm small and I have no confidence and think I'm a shit.' Because you just can't do that on stage. You're not supposed to, and probably you don't have much confidence, and you do think you're a little piece of shit, or else you wouldn't have gotten a rock band together in the first place.

Musically the song hinges on a glistering guitar figure concocted by Jimmy, for which the axeman quite properly received a composer's credit.

Subsequently a massive worldwide hit, 'Brass In Pocket' has become the sound of 1980 and beyond, a great primer on The Pretenders' musical flexibility and vow never to be straight-jacketed by any one style – no matter how comfortable the band were with both crunching, punchy rock and sublimely classy, intelligent pop.

'Lovers Of Today' 5.51 (Hynde)
This epic song demonstrates how well The Pretenders and their leader can move from major-to-minor-key-and-back-again in the service of shifting mood and emotion. It's another of Chrissie Hynde's very best, her vocal performance among her most impassioned. She funnels every last microgram of feeling through her ever-delicate vibrato, realising both a lullaby that might soothe a child and a ballad, more assertive but no less caring, aimed at reassuring her equally innocent man. Indeed (if not in fact), these recipients of the singer's ardour might be two sides of a single personality. He's a composite man-child, around whose vulnerabilities Chrissie's every instinct, despite outward appearances, is to create a protective cocoon against the simple, petrifying jeopardies of infancy, and against the complex assumptions and prejudices of the adult world:

> I put my arms around my baby
> I said hush, hush, hush, hush, baby sleep tight now
> Hush, hush, hush baby, sleep
> 'Cause all of the birds start to sing, every time babies dream
> All of the birds start to sing.
> Nobody wants to see
> Lovers of today happy, so assume they're going to part
> Nobody wants to be with someone
> So afraid they'll be left with a broken heart.

Underlining the duality, the song toggles Chrissie's plaintive voice, accompanied by a sweet guitar arpeggio, with a powerful change as the rhythm section dives in: a dynamic gearshift that recurs brilliantly throughout the song. The singer's messaging strengthens as the object of her affection morphs from child to grown-up. In the middle eight, the musicians intensify, Jimmy's swirling solo introducing a searing atonality to an arrangement that is, by now, all-powerful. As the solo decays at 4.41, Chrissie's double-tracked vocal returns to pull together the two archetypes, baby and man, before the song fades off into a devastating coda and the singer's enigmatic closing words:

> I tried to talk to you baby
> No no no, I'll never feel
> Like a man in a man's world.

'Mystery Achievement' 5.24 (Hynde)
Heralded by a mighty 4/4 from Martin Chambers' snare, the combined bass essences of James Jamerson, Muff Winwood and Barry Adamson inspire Pete Farndon to torpedo his instrument through a graphite pile and out the other side. 'Mystery Achievement' goes nuclear from the start, marshalling Stevie Wonder's 'Uptight', Spencer Davis' 'Keep On Running' and Magazine's 'The Light Pours Out Of Me' in a cone-crushing reminder of the power surge always promised by The Pretenders once they withdraw all the control rods. The whole band are slaves to the song's frantic 139 bpm, which never lets up even for a beautifully fluid middle break from Jimmy, the guitar loosening Martin's lolloping fills like an industrial grease gun.

Once again Chrissie delivers her quickfire lyrics torrentially and without pause. The mystery achievement might be the acclaim that awaits; while success will assail the writer at pace after 'Brass In Pocket' goes ballistic, stardom is still an unknown quantity at the time of 'Mystery Achievement's composition. But, surprise, surprise, her confidence is high; if there is doubt, it comes a poor second to ballsy assertiveness, and she's in no mood to be hurried. Mentally, she's already checked in at the Hyatt House and chucked the TVs into the swimming pool. But whatever happens will be in her time and no-one else's, with plenty of space to have fun and 'get out on the floor'.

Perhaps the mystery achievement is more personal, sealed from the obvious trappings of rock stardom; certainly she could be addressing another party. But whatever the nature of her uncertain goal, she's cool about the possibility of failure, unwilling to cry over spilt milk. A final appropriate reminder that nothing is too serious closes the book on one of rock's greatest maiden albums:

> Mystery achievement
> Where's my sandy beach?
> Yeah, I had my dreams like everybody else
> But they're out of reach
> I said right out of reach
> I could ignore you
> Your demands are unending
> I got no tears on my ice cream
> But you know me, I love pretending.

Associated
Bonus CD Included With 2006 Reissue Of Pretenders
'Cuban Slide'/'Porcelain'/'The Phone Call' (demo)/'The Wait' (demo)/'I Can't Control Myself' (demo)/'Swinging London'/'Brass In Pocket' (demo)/'Kid' (demo)/'Stop Your Sobbing' (demo)/'Tequila' (demo)/'Nervous But Shy'/'I Need Somebody' (live)/'Mystery Achievement' (live)/'Precious' (live)/'Tattooed Love Boys' (live)/'Sabre Dance' (live)

Selected Reviews
'Cuban Slide' 4.32 (Hynde)
The omission of 'Cuban Slide' from *Pretenders* would have been less mystery than actionable in the CD age. With the album's 50-minute vinyl cup already running over with outstanding material, this great song was consigned to *Extended Play*, the interim 1981 non-UK EP, and thereafter to the 2006 digital reissue of *Pretenders*. With typically Hyndeian contrariness, 'Cuban Slide' – the dance is already referenced in 'Mystery Achievement' – shuns the time-honoured salsa rhythms that normally sashay Havana night-owls into the small hours. Instead, Martin's blockhouse toms and Pete's farting bass burst straight into a Bo Diddley hambone – with its tremolo guitar effects, it could be Jerome Green, The Duchess and the Mississippi master himself – until 2.05, when Jimmy goes somewhere else again, adroitly patching in a repeating, memorably shimmering Beatles/Byrds Rickenbacker figure. He even throws in a couple of block chords that wouldn't embarrass Pete Townshend, before essaying a middle solo that simply glows. Lyrically, Chrissie uses dance as a metaphor, a melancholic expression of uncertainty rather at odds with the tune's cheerful mood.

'Porcelain' 3.52 (Hynde)
Pack up the bone china: cranked up to eleven, 'Porcelain' would be banging enough to smash concrete. In this case, the eponymous vitrified pottery comprises a restroom floor, possibly in some nameless hotel, upon which Chrissie has laid her aching head as she comes around from whatever ju-ju mixture got her through the night. Room service arrives at the end with her 'private order'. Provenance is uncertain: either she wrote the song during The Pretenders' first or second US tour, or for an earlier London session in the band's infancy.

'Nervous But Shy' 1.45 (The Pretenders)
A throwaway instrumental that sounds like one of those impromptu fillers rock bands trot out onstage while they wait for the lights to be fixed. An example of the uncanny empathy between young musicians on the cusp of global acclaim? Or needless wear to a spool of Ampex and a sound engineer's patience? You choose.

'Swinging London' 1.54 (The Pretenders)
Another short, undistinguished pop-rock instrumental. It's so soaked in the early 1960s it could be The Mojos doing the soundcheck before opening for Gerry & The Pacemakers at the Cavern Club.

'Suicide' 3.32 (Hynde)
'What makes you so sure death can cure your fear?' Chrissie enquires of an unknown unfortunate. She could be talking down a friend from a fate worse

than cocktails with the Heavy Bikers. Such were some of the folk she was hanging with in 1977, when this rough-as-old-boots demo was probably recorded.

'I Can't Control Myself' 4.23 (Reg Presley)
Some accounts, Chrissie's among them, would have this a punked-up version of The Troggs' deathless hit from 1966. But the ghost of the great Reg Presley haunts only dimly this early demo, for its heavily deconstructed lyrics and arrangement effectively render a different song. Given The Troggs were, in essence, one of Britain's first successful punk bands – as a pretty-boy pop star, the stout Reg squinted down from the same unlikely firmament as fellow rubes Freddie Garrity and Tiny Tim – heaven knows the original was sneery enough. Now vigorously sped up and turned inside-out by the pre-Pretenders at Dave Hill's seminal Regent Sound session, this charmingly tinny 'I Can't Control Myself' evidences a rock group in its infancy, straining at the reins, ready to take on the world.

'Tequila' 5.19 (Hynde)
Not the old saxophone workout by The Champs, but The Pretenders' demo of the country-&-western parody that would eventually surface, scrubbed and thankfully truncated, on 1994's fine *Last Of The Independents*. If there's a model for Chrissie's lament for lost love over too much cactus juice, the closest might be Willie Nelson's 'Time Of The Preacher'; although truthfully, the C&W genre being what it is, she must have heard dozens of similarly lachrymose ditties on the car radio during her mid-1970s Arizona road-trip, when she wrote the song.

'Do I Love You' 2.57 (Spector/Poncia/Andreoli)
Yes, this *is* the epic of that name originally by The Ronettes. This was recorded by Chrissie in 1978, accompanied by The Sunshine Boys (cunningly disguised as Sex Pistols Steve Jones and Paul Cook) in what sounds like an aircraft hanger. The musicians don't quite scale the soaring wall of sound of Phil Spector's astounding original, but for a demo its rough authenticity is striking. Along with 'Sabre Dance' (below), 'Do I Love You' makes this *Pretenders* bonus sequence worthwhile.

'I Need Somebody' 3.48 (Rudy Martinez)
Ah, those heady days when, for a Saturday morning radio audience, a successful pop group would run through ordinary B-list songs that might be lucky to see release as album fillers. The Pretenders do the honours for Kid Jensen's Radio One show in July 1979, with a decent club mover accented by stabbing guitar, insistent single-note electric piano, Martin's piledriving drums and a nicely cluttered solo from Jimmy. Of the song's provenance, composer Martinez was (slightly) better known as the ? in Question Mark & The

Mysterians, a garage band out of Saginaw, Michigan, who scored a number one on *Billboard* in 1966 with the proto-punk '96 Tears'. This would have loomed large in Chrissie Hynde's Midwest teenage fancies. As a tip of the hat to the primitive creative forces that shaped the singer, it's entirely fine.

'Sabre Dance' 3.51 (Aram Khachaturian)
Recorded live at the Marquee Club in 1979, a truly deranged version of the Georgian composer's famous ballet from the Gayane Suite: a classical piece everyone's heard but few can name. Having long idolised Dave Edmunds, Jimmy Scott will have known inside-out the six-minute maelstrom with which Edmunds' power trio, Love Sculpture, scored a surprise singles hit in 1968. Here Jimmy takes a lip-biting guitar hero's solo at the same crazed velocity as the Cardiff maestro's, driven hard by Martin's murderous snare, while Chrissie mans the mic and attempts to upstage her guitarist with occasional dismembered quotes from 'Stop Your Sobbing'. The instrumental abruptly fades after 3.51, suggesting it was longer on the night (Love Sculpture's unedited album version exceeded 11 minutes). You probably had to be there, but 'Sabre Dance' is great fun, and an example of how good Honeyman-Scott could be when given the space to let rip.

Pretenders II (1981)

Personnel
Chrissie Hynde: guitars, vocals
James Honeyman-Scott: guitars, keyboards, vocals
Pete Farndon: bass, vocals
Martin Chambers: drums, vocals
Chris Mercer: tenor saxophone
Henry Lowther: trumpet
Jim Wilson: trumpet
Geoff Bryant: French horn
Chris Thomas: odds & ends
Produced at Wessex Studios, London; Pathe Marconi Studios, Paris, by Chris Thomas
Engineers: Bill Price, Jeremy Green, Jon Walls
Released: August 1981
Highest chart position: UK: 7, US: 10

> I bluff a lot of it, and I've never told the rest of the group ... that I can't work out those fucking times at all. I just do it my own way.
> **James Honeyman-Scott, Jas Obrecht, 1981**

Most successful artists give it two or three albums at least before the difficulties set in. The impact of The Pretenders' first, however, alongside the hit singles, incendiary live act and media brouhaha, saw the band wilting under rock 'n' roll's two most common and virulent symptoms of hubris – drugs and money – even before they were studio-bound for their second.

Drugs, of course, were a given. No sooner had *Pretenders* rifled into *Billboard*'s chart early in 1980 than the band were off on a five-month tour of the US, with all of its attendant marketing opportunities for backstage entrepreneurs and hangers-on. The tour was split by a European multi-city break and a stint at Wessex Studios. 'Three weeks down the pan,' fretted Chris Thomas, bemoaning the unpreparedness of his habitually revelling clients, whose lack of material and overall sense of disorder helped realise just one new recording.

In an interview with *Melody Maker*'s Allan Jones in 1999, shortly before the release of The Pretenders' seventh studio album, *¡Viva El Amor!*, Chrissie spoke tellingly of the intolerable tensions that snapped the original band and the pressures, more often than not dope-related, that bore down so damagingly on provincial *naifs* Jimmy and Pete:

> I hated people using drugs as a way of getting close to the band. So, I always went off on my own. But ... Jimmy was a speed freak. Cocaine was too expensive for us when we started. And there was always that smack element hanging around. When Johnny Thunders & The Heartbreakers

came over to London, smack really became the cool thing. Pete was absolutely mesmerised by Johnny Thunders. When [Thunders] left a blood-soaked tea towel in Pete's kitchen, that to Pete was an example of rock 'n' roll genius. The writing was on the wall from then on. But, hey, these were just guys from Hereford. They didn't know what hit them. It was too much too soon for them. But for me – I'd been crawling in the gutter for years. It wasn't too soon for me at all. But, shit, they'd never even been to America. And when they did get there ... they thought it was the greatest. They didn't throw themselves into it; they fucking *hurled* themselves into it.

Pete Farndon had been balancing on the rim of a substance-filled black hole for several months, gobbling whizz and scag like egg and chips at the Blue Boar. Having already helped terminate Pete's romance with Chrissie, the excesses were now chiselling away at brothers-in-arms Martin and Jimmy. The more Pete used, the less his bass playing amounted to anything, and with it he risked funnelling away the band's hard-won unity. This was not lost on Jimmy, who, for all the guitarist's own partialities, remained utterly committed to The Pretenders' music. As the record execs demanded new product, the riotous travelling a hazy memory of tour buses, bar brawls and backstage ribaldry, the band saw its heart all but burned out. Farndon, the once happy-go-lucky country boy from Hereford, was blackening to a violent, smack-fixated wraith. 'Pete's junkie persona had taken over and was inhabiting him, like a demonic possession', Chrissie wrote in *Reckless*. 'His best friends couldn't find him behind the sallow mask.'

At least the band weren't forced into conventional crime; The Pretenders' hedonism was bankrolled by the substantial brass in pocket from touring and record sales. But satisfying an industry beast whose appetite grows proportionately with the fortunes of a rock band relies on new songs – and, as the relentless partying militated against on-the-road creativity, Chrissie hadn't much in the pantry.

Some of *Pretenders II* was cut at Pathe Marconi Studios in Paris. Hynde preferred to record in England, but her three English co-workers, awash in new money, suddenly discovered an urgent need to steer clear of the Inland Revenue. More positively – for tax avoidance doesn't normally inspire good rock music unless you're The Rolling Stones – producer Thomas wanted to leverage Pathe Marconi's famed drum acoustics. With the shortfall in new material and a world tour pending, the band had to get their skates on – and haste in itself was its own brake on creativity. As the clock ran down on Pathe Marconi, the outcome was seven songs in varying states of repair and a pause in Thomas's involvement. Expecting to finish The Pretenders' new album by Christmas 1980, the ever-busy producer had other urgent business with Elton John. By the following spring, however, the band and Thomas were able to reconnect. After that, the only way was Wessex.

The dearth of songs and general disarray had silenced any immediate talk of a second album. But since the first, the band had managed one of their finest singles, 'Talk Of The Town' b/w 'Cuban Slide' ('Stop Your Sobbing' in the US), which peaked in the UK at number 8 in March 1980. Another, 'Message Of Love' b/w 'Porcelain', would be a British number 11 in February 1981. The group also resurrected the venerable EP, or extended play: a halfway-house release that was longer than a single, shorter than an album and a convenient way to sweeten the suits between proper long-players. The imaginatively titled *Extended Play* gathered the abovementioned A- and (English) B-sides, along with 'Precious'; the latter a fierce reading of the opening song from *Pretenders* taped in Central Park in August 1980, and a tantalising glimpse of how efficiently the original quartet might have saddled up another old rock 'n' roll warhorse, the live album. (In 1982, unearthed as a bonus disc with a remastered *Pretenders II* in 2006, Warners issued the promo-only *Live At The Santa Monica Civic 1981*, featuring a typical setlist of the time.) Unreleased in the UK, *Extended Play* reached number 29 in Australia and number 27 on US *Billboard*, despite the 12" vinyl format leaving Americans scratching their heads. 'It looked like an album, and people bought it as such,' Chrissie told Chris Salewicz. 'So it went into the LP charts. And we felt really hard-pressed *not* to put all of those songs on [the new] album.' The leader was adamant that 'Message Of Love', in particular, would be included on *Pretenders II*. 'That's what we'd recorded it for ... Essentially, [the EP] was a big cockup.'

That the second album eventually delivered on the promise of the first evinces a hunger to make great music as yet unslaked by the all-too-human weaknesses of young, rich, naive musicians. *Pretenders II* turned out similar in structure to the earlier record: an exciting mix of angry, angular riffery, surprising signatures, eccentric scansion, wry observation, nonchalant put-downs and acidic character assassination. The two singles the band prepared earlier were included and remain among their best. A third, sole survivor from the otherwise barren first three weeks at Wessex Studios, once again bore the imprimatur of one Raymond Douglas Davies; 'I Go To Sleep', only ever a demo by The Kinks, was a gorgeous love ballad, Chrissie proving she could be as tender as she was elsewhere abrasive. Who could she have been thinking of?

Davies, of course, had loomed large for Chrissie's younger self as pop icon and teen crush. In September 1980, Head Kink and Great Pretender were united by a mutual friend at Trax, a trendy music-biz nightclub on New York City's Upper West Side. Chrissie was soon stepping out with the new boyfriend while still living with the old one, a situation made even more byzantine by the ever-more extreme amusements of her now ex-squeeze, Pete. Needless to say, any pally chest bumps between the two alphas – one a reclusive, self-possessed songwriting genius, the other a talented but prematurely self-damaged jack-the-lad – would always look like a pair of Sumo wrestlers having at it in an exhibition match. As for the other happy couple, Chrissie and Ray were quickly exhibiting all the patience and sweet reason of Scott and

Zelda Fitzgerald, demonstrating their love for each other with as many heavy objects as they could throw from Big Apple hotel windows.

There was more: when Ray invited Chrissie to join The Kinks onstage at a big outdoor festival on the West Coast, his brother Dave spat in her face (the guitarist's justification, when later quizzed by a fan, demonstrated similar chivalry: 'who wouldn't?'). One night Ray, who frequently attended Pretenders shows, was lamped by Farndon or Scott or both, a deed related as much to the tribal protective instincts of Pretenders' manhood as to a reflexive, proxy retaliation for the spitting incident. As for the younger Davies, who professed supernatural leanings, Dave was asked by their sister Peggy to investigate haunted knavery in a house shared by Ray and Chrissie. Apparently Raymond could commune with the spirits with the best: 'I went upstairs into the attic to tell the ghost that it no longer had any place [here],' he told biographer Johnny Rogan, 'but Chrissie was still terrified.' However, Dave's bell, book and candle proved redundant; the amateur exorcist's report ID'd the spook as nothing more than the psychic energy set free by Chrissie and Ray, their constant bickering perhaps proof that you should never meet your heroes in the flesh, still less set sail with them on a choppy four-year love affair. The pair planned to marry; come the happy day – timed, it was said, to coincide with the conception of their child – such was their public display of enmity that an exasperated registrar called the whole thing off.

More fractious inter-band messing summed up a tumultuous 1981 world tour in support of *Pretenders II*. In April, Jimmy wed a Texan model called, rather wonderfully, Peggy Sue Fender. Marriage might have briefly nudged the guitarist towards amphetamine detox, but since he could now afford as much cocaine as he wanted the benefits were annulled. He was also drinking heavily, enough to suffer a collapse with diagnosed cirrhosis in mid-tour. A tired and emotional Chrissie kicked out a Memphis police cruiser's window while under arrest for panning a nightclub owner – it was coming to something when that model of sobriety Johnny Thunders, sporting a purple lip from a doped-out fall downstairs, counselled Hynde to get her act together – while by now Pete's veins must have looked and felt like congealed Plasticene.

The Pretenders were doing a stand-up job of group-wide self-immolation, and for perhaps the first time in rock history it couldn't be blamed on the drummer. Even the stoical Chambers, himself recently married, had his problems: that autumn, following a quarrel with a bedside lamp in a Philadelphia hotel, Martin lacerated a tendon in his hand, an injury serious enough to warrant immediate surgery and scuppering his playing for several weeks. Rather than replace the musician who so intuitively grasped how his leader's polybonkers song structures played out onstage, the band decided to postpone dates in the US and Canada while he recovered. An offer to understudy by the ex-Vanilla Fudge engine-house Carmine Appice was politely declined.

In contrast with much of its content's easy pep and punch, the cover of *Pretenders II* unwittingly plays to the doubts that attend every successful band's 'difficult' second album. Snapper Gavin Cochrane channels David Bailey's moodily magnificent, rock-stars-as-South-London-gangsters portraiture from the second Stones album and fetches up with a heavily airbrushed and depressing murk. The *Pretenders* sleeve's stoner lifeforce is suddenly absent, the group now as animated as Madame Tussauds rejects. Chrissie and an extravagantly pompadoured Pete (dressed respectively as CEO of a moderately successful Dundee haulage firm and Grand Ole Opry doorman – albeit one aglow with what Hynde described as 'the green pallor of smack') stand stiff as cuckoo-clock figurines, bookending a sulky guitarist and a drummer now less scruffy estate agent than vaudevillian spiv. The shot does the band neither justice nor favours.

As if sensing musicians recovering from recent bloodletting – although much worse was to come – English critics circled like starving sharks, tearing strips from an album that was actually very much better than anyone following the band's behaviour could have predicted. In the US, however, with Bruce Springsteen and Nils Lofgren among the rock nabobs queueing to join The Pretenders onstage, it was appropriate that critical balance should be redressed by a posh broadsheet: 'If it is a more conservative album than its predecessor, it is also, musically speaking, a more substantial one,' intoned *The New York Times*. 'Each of the songs is packed with instrumental and vocal detail, and while some of the arrangements on the first album trumpeted their daring, on the new LP, the seams simply don't show.'

Unsurprisingly sales weren't shabby: *Pretenders II* spent 30 weeks on the UK albums chart, peaking at number seven, while America, having now sussed what this badass vixen from the plains was up to with these whey-faced limeys, sent it to number ten on *Billboard* and later awarded it an RIAA gold record.

'The Adultress' 3.58 (Hynde)

Like its predecessor, *Pretenders II* kicks away from the starting blocks like Usain Bolt. This time it's a far from Precious confessional, managing to be perceptive, pugnacious and poignant all at once. In less nuanced, more binary times, the narrator would have been chided as a floozy: a handy receptacle for clandestine, joylessly exchanged fluids, her infidelity perfunctory and symbolic only of the shameless sexual betrayal of an innocent. But as with so many of Chrissie Hynde's songs, such a zero-sum dismissal sorely underrates the subtleties of 'The Adultress'. While the subject's inability to say 'no' racks her with guilt, there's an inevitability to it all, prompting little more than a shrug of the shoulders:

> I'm the adulteress
> But I didn't want to be and I'm convenient
> And I make good tea

> I stand accused
> Of the worst crime in history
> That's my mystery
> I'm the adulteress
> I go to the park
> With a bag of crumbs for the birds
> That's where we meet without words
> He takes my hand
> And stares into the wood
> There's nothing to understand
> It's understood
> I'm the adulteress.

By the end the furtive deception broadens, perhaps played out in regular arboreal trysts with the same lover (who may have been the still-married Ray Davies). Though her conscience might quietly be troubling her, the lyrics suggest similar pleasures may be tasted by others, either as emotional outfall or as straightforward business transactions. Aggressive and sad in equal measure, Chrissie's *Belle de Jour* sets out her stall:

> Look at the fool
> Made up to go out
> She's desperate and lonely
> But she's puttin' it about
> Look at the spinster
> Comin' down off the shelf
> She's in love and she hates herself
> Don't try to stop me
> Don't get in my way
> It's too late
> I've made my play
> Does misery love company
> I'll be in the bar
> You'll find me.

If her words come wrapped in paradox – Chrissie's half-sung, half-spoken, quiveringly lower-lipped delivery is at once threatening, defensive and submissive – the music is all jagged, throbbing, percussive hostility. 'The Adultress' feels like what 'Space Invader' had been heading towards as soon as words and some studious refinement were seeded into the first album's powerhouse instrumental.

In a 1981 interview with guitar critic Jas Obrecht, Jimmy Scott talked of the unusual demands imposed upon his playing by Chrissie's idiosyncratic approach to rhythm and metre:

If I come in a bar too late, [the band] are used to me coming in a bar too late, and they think that's how I play. But it's because I've missed where she's come in ... We've done a track called 'The Adultress' where I come in a beat too late because I cannot count the timing, and they think it's great: 'Oh, that's Jimmy's style.' And the fact is, I don't know where she comes in with it. So I just bluff it and hope for the best.

'Bad Boys Get Spanked' 4.07 (Hynde)

In another echo of *Pretenders*, the crystal-meth rush of 'Tattooed Love Boys' is drawn off for an unambiguous assertion of feminine command and control. Is the bad boy the same one so heartlessly cuckolded by The Adultress? If so, Chrissie feels no need for the closeted guilt, spiced with fragile nonchalance, of the earlier song; she's having his eyes as recompense for his own weaknesses and, perhaps, because one (or both) even enjoys the experience – the former cited as the reason for the latter. Her reproaches intensify as the narrative proceeds. In places her delivery is almost orgasmic, her punctuating screams and the occasional whipcrack turning the song into an exposition of a sadomasochistic tumble between Venus in Furs and her luckless yet compliant Severin.

It's tempting to see the pattern established on the first album: the hostile maneater turned up to 11, her male compadres buzzing around her like angry workers protecting their queen. Yet, there's no sense of formulaic laziness merely to fulfil quota; the band are smoking like a Kuwaiti oil fire, Scotty's fresh guitar chords trying their best to rein in Chrissie's reverbed vocals and gasps of ecstasy over Martin's relentless shuffle beat.

'Message Of Love' 3.25 (Hynde)

The album's third song is four-to-the-floor simplicity itself: just two chords and no chorus, with a spiffing chromatic change and some great instrumental breaks. With its title lifted from Jimi Hendrix (by Chrissie's admission: 'I always want to pay tribute to my heroes'), musically 'Message Of Love' is punky, although its sentiments square more with luvved-up hippie unity than with scornful aggression. The singer is apparently newly in love, basking in the afterglow, perhaps on a happy pill or two.

But 'Message Of Love' is less the narcotic after the amphetamine than the strawberries and cream after the asparagus. The savage lashing from Chrissie's tongue (and other ordnance) of 'Bad Boys' has softened; give or take the odd quotation from Oscar Wilde, the lyrics are guileless and reminiscent of many a 1960s hit. More broadly, the song is about caring for each other. 'I think we're social creatures', Chrissie told *Blue Railroad* in 2011. 'We have to look after each other because if we were supposed to be alone, there would be only one person on the planet.' Can this really be the same woman last seen straddling her supine partner with a six-inch stiletto heel to his jugular?

The perfidy of the first track and the bondage-chic of the second have settled into flirtatious poptimism pitched squarely at chart success, which it justly achieved. Leading the charge from *Pretenders II*, 'Message Of Love' hit number five on the US *Billboard* Mainstream Rock chart and number 11 in the UK. (Somewhat overplaying the romanticism – as if US rock biz suits worried that the band, and Chrissie in particular, might be too abrasive for pop fans in Rubber City – the single was released in February 1981, just in time for Valentine's Day.)

'Message Of Love' was largely constructed from scratch in Paris. Recording a brand-new, unrehearsed song in the studio was unusual, as Martin explained to J. J. Jackson of *MTV* later that year:

> We have done that once and that was 'Message Of Love'. Chrissie likes to come to the band when she has a song finished in her mind, but this time, she hadn't really finished it, and so we just rehearsed it already set up in the studio and it was on tape in two hours.

'I Go To Sleep' 2.57 (Ray Davies)

Few singers of the past 40 years have matched Chrissie Hynde's effortless facility to toggle between punk derision and naked sensitivity while freighting every word, be it spat or quivered, with equal resonance. Following the razor assault of the album's two openers and the brightening positivity of the third, the mood slides slinkily towards the boudoir, its aphrodisiac fragrance themed by a memorable French horn figure.

The world and her aunt were covering 'I Go To Sleep' ages before a 2011 reissue of *Kinda Kinks* finally set free the composer's original: a charming 1965 demo by Ray Davies accompanying himself at a hesitant piano. Like its predecessor, The Kinks' second album was rushed – the band had heavy touring commitments – so it was over to Cher, on her introductory solo LP, *All I Really Want To Do* (1965), to first bring Davies' gently exquisite serenade into the public domain. This was followed in short order by a failed single by The Applejacks, then Peggy Lee, then Lesley Duncan, after which Wikipedia lists at least 24 more readings. And while this author cannot vouch for every entry in an extensive canon of sometimes obscure artists, it's Cher's maiden effort that seems most closely to accord with the version made famous by The Pretenders.

Both singers' low contraltos are uncannily similar. But Chrissie's yearning vibrato is better accented than Cher's, soaked in the vulnerability so crucial to a song that sits far from the aggressive sulphate flash of early Pretenders at full throttle – and from The Kinks', come to that. Ms Sarkisian's delivery is that of a hip but mainstream torch singer knowingly celebrating some of the era's most popular songwriters – Davies, Dylan, Jackie de Shannon, Cher's hubby Sonny Bono – and feeling well chuffed to be doing so. As interpreted by Peggy Lee – the 'Queen of American Pop Music' was gifted the song by an admiring Davies – the lyrics are dispensed mechanically, the emotion clipped back to a staccato indifference, all suggesting managerial edict and the notion that Her Majesty did not reciprocate her assumed court composer's regard. When His Kinkness wrote the song, Ray was tarrying in a hospital corridor as his first wife produced the couple's baby daughter. Given provenance and sensitivity, to approach 'I Go To Sleep' with anything other than hushed reverence would seem a crime against maternity.

Following Geoff Bryant's luxuriant horn intro, Chrissie is happily, longingly woozy and passionate, lingering so much on the 'sleep' in the chorus that she might have been recording from her bed. On her watch, the song evokes less a father's love for his newborn than a woman's for her man. But by 1981, she and Ray were an item; any song penned by her beau could only have been rendered by The Pretenders with the utmost affection. Backed with live versions of 'The English Roses' and 'Louie Louie' (both recorded at Santa Monica Civic on 4 September 1981), 'I Go To Sleep' was released as a UK single on 14 November, peaking at number seven.

'Birds Of Paradise' 4.15 (Hynde)
The tender mood continues to defuse the aggression of *Pretenders II*'s first two songs. In a stately waltz time, Jimmy's up-and-down arpeggios resonate with more romance than an Emily Dickinson quatrain, even as his soloing in the break and Martin's assertive drumming punch up the drama at just the right moments. 'Birds Of Paradise' could have been written for any of the great 1960s torch singers, yet Chrissie proves she has no need of such geniuses of emotional interpretation as, say, Ronnie Spector or Dusty Springfield. She invests her own words with wrenching sensitivity, a force-field of passion radiated by her now beautifully controlled vibrato: a vocal technique that's teasingly harder to master than it seems. Many can do it, but few do it well; with 'Birds Of Paradise' and other early power ballads by The Pretenders, Chrissie proves she's the one to beat.

The song's subject is uncertain. If it's about Pete, Chrissie recalls what she and the bassist shared before the affection was eaten away by the stoned termites' nest of the music business. It's worth remembering that the star-crossed love affair had been as much the band's foundational impetus as any individual ambition: 'Much of the chemistry and the passion of The Pretenders was due to the intensity of the relationship between Chrissie and Pete,' wrote Chris Salewicz, 'and to their fiery energy that thereby fuelled the birth of the group.'

'Birds Of Paradise' is far from a standard-issue love song, however. In the second verse, Chrissie conjures a childhood exemplar of how a grown-up love affair might play out:

When I was a little girl
With clay horses and lambs on the shelf

> I caught frogs in ditches, listened for elves
> My friends and I had a world unto ourselves
> No grownups could find us when we
> Made our plans so secretly
> To run away and fly to be
> With the two birds of paradise.

The melancholic air suggests the dream could not be sustained. By the end, the singer is craving her errant companion's forgiveness, a position less counter-intuitive than it appears. As we've heard in the sentiments of 'Up The Neck' and 'Tattooed Love Boys', Chrissie is, at heart, a conservative woman. She's too ready to turn a battered cheek, explaining away the maltreatment meted out by a boorish and even violent lover as somehow her fault, or simply another facet of the hackneyed, boy-meets-girl scheme of things. Here she wishes back that uncomplicated childhood dream, where paradise never ends, the rock 'n' roll nightmare a figment of a fevered imagination:

> Please don't forget
> Do forgive me
> I still have something you did give me
> Come into my dream with me and dream
> Oh dream of paradise.

'Talk Of The Town' 2.44 (Hynde)

The title of this fine song, slightly shorter than its April 1980 release as The Pretenders' fourth single, remembers a storied London nightclub, which in 1983 was handed back its original 1900 name, the Hippodrome, before its closure in 2009. As the Talk Of The Town, the nitespot hosted talents as diverse as the Temptations, Dusty Springfield, Lonnie Donegan and Frank Sinatra.

It's tempting to imagine 'Talk Of The Town', as many did at the time, as a paean to Ray Davies. After all, what could get a town gossiping faster than a romance between London's hottest rock star and the genius behind 'Waterloo Sunset'? In a 1999 acoustic set for the *Songwriters' Circle* BBC TV show, Chrissie finally explained the roots of a track musically based, according to Jimmy, on a Beatles chord:

> I had in mind this kid who used to stand outside the sound checks on our first tour, and I never spoke to him. I remember the last time I saw him, I just left him standing in the snow. I never had anything to say to him, and I kind of wrote 'Talk Of The Town' for him.

Chrissie has been reluctant to talk, with the town or with anybody else, about her relationship with Ray. (The feelings are cordially mutual.) It's therefore possible that the song's subject conflates Davies, both in his unreachable mid-1960s persona and as a bona fide lover 15 years on, with the unknown but clearly attractive fan. In his own way, this kid is unavailable; despite her predatory reputation, Chrissie had her own weaknesses; she wasn't always inclined to hit on a stranger out of the blue. This might especially be true if he reminded her of a teenage crush she'd idolised since forever and whom she was now, almost counter-intuitively, dating. I know! As so often with a Hynde lyric, it's ambiguous.

The song closes wistfully, as if she became better acquainted with the stranger than she let on in 1999 but allowed him to slip through her fingers:

> Oh but it's hard to live by the rules
> I never could and still never do
> The rules and such never bothered you
> You call the shots and they follow
> I watch you still from a distance then go
> Back to my room, you never know
> I want you, I want you but now
> Who's the talk of the town?

What of Jimmy's Beatles notion? Bright as a button on Lord Kitchener's tunic, with gorgeous guitar chords and arpeggios, 'Talk Of The Town' twinkles with mid-period Fabs, its simple but memorable melody underpinned by Pete's stolid bass. The rhythm section even pushes The Pretenders further towards late-model Beatles c1969; with a satisfying heaviness sitting sweetly with a pop sensibility easily the match of, say, 'Kid', the guitar flavourings evoke George Harrison from the majestic second side of *Abbey Road*.

Among the many to be exercised by 'Talk Of The Town' was Pretenders fangirl Shirley Manson. In 1998, Manson's band, Garbage, repurposed the refrain for their third single, 'Special', which hit number 15 in the UK and number 52 on US *Billboard*. After Shirley sought permission to ad-lib the lyric – the American band's record company attorneys insisted – Chrissie agreed without hesitation, requesting neither royalties nor credit. Her friend and admirer's respect was clearly reciprocated: '[Shirley can sample] my sounds, my voice or indeed my very ass.'

'Pack It Up' 3.51 (Hynde/Honeyman-Scott)

'You guys are the pits of the world!' So did John McEnroe's momentary lapse of reason in June 1981 infamously turn the starchy green blazers of Wimbledon's old guard a livid purple. Two months later, Chrissie Hynde, hailed by the tennis god (and sometime guitarist) as the greatest female rock star since Janis Joplin, channels her fellow rebel and new bestie as she repeats, at the beginning of 'Pack It Up', McEnroe's excoriation of blinkered officialdom.

The couplet 'That's showbiz, big boy/You've got to be cruel to be kind' suggests a sly tilt at Nick Lowe. Was this because Basher had the nerve to decline the production detail on The Pretenders' first album? But the tirade feels too splenetically vicious to be aimed specifically at an ex-lover with whom Chrissie remained pals, despite Nick's professional doubts over her early demos. Some believe 'Pack It Up' is a breakup song – the sentiments bear this out – while others detect something broader. There are veiled references to her home state and the passing of time; the singer could be venting at a composite of ex-boyfriends and the more vacuous entities strewn around the record business like coke-stained 'C' notes on a studio floor. Given McEnroe's original taunt was pitched at those who regulate his own trade, perhaps the targets of Chrissie's vitriol are to be found among the besuited umpires of the music industry. Whoever the unfortunate victim(s) may be, Chrissie gives no quarter; with half-spoken glee, the singer lets loose a murderous drive-by that's both savage and comical:

> I may be a skunk
> But you're a piece of junk
> And furthermore I don't like your trousers
> Your appalling taste in women
> And what about your mind
> Your insipid record collection
> That dumb home video center
> The usual pornography...

Can't you just see Chrissie gleefully chucking those horrid flares and third-generation reprints of *Debbie Does Dallas* from a second-floor window? The band hammer out a simple, hard and insistent riff with little let-up over co-writer Jimmy's shimmering guitar underlay. The pounding rhythm relaxes for a relatively restrained middle before Chrissie's climactic reminder, lest we forget the overriding emotions amid the percussive audial gale: 'You're the pits of the world!'

'Waste Not Want Not' 3.45 (Hynde)

Two albums in, and Chrissie Hynde's acuity as a sexual politician and poignant chronicler of her own tragi-comic past was beyond dispute. However, as numerous interviewers and journalists could attest, she rarely held back when it came to questioning the world beyond the parochial. So it was somehow inevitable that a Pretenders song would eventually address the environment and its wilful despoilers.

With 'Waste Not Want Not', Chrissie is lyrically on point, if inconsistently. At best she's the activist in the size-ten Doc Martens, shaking her fist, waving a banner and supergluing herself to a JCB (life later imitated art: in 2013, Chrissie's daughter Natalie would do something similar). Elsewhere, however, the angry polemic fades to a resigned lament, her wordplay only occasionally as forthright as we know this vocal and near-lifelong vegetarian to be. That her barbs should be so leisurely deployed is due more to a discouraging framework than the lyrical imagery within it. For musically 'Waste Not Want Not' is one of *Pretenders II*'s least interesting tracks, a ponderously throwaway reggae that seems to end before it's begun.

Pete's bass grumbles belligerently as the singer identifies what's at stake:

> See the networks of concrete and steel
> They've no mystery but what they reveal
> Tells a story of a future that's void
> Of the beauty and the majesty of life on Earth
> Is meant to be.

A later-model Hynde would have smelted errant industrialists and funnelled them through outfalls of their own slurry, toughening up the musical language in support of her withering contempt. Here, however, the song's excoriations sometimes come across more as pleas than demands, her rhetorical punches pulled or neutralised by the dull setting. She appeals to the better side of human nature, firmly but politely asking the guilty to reconsider and moderate their misbehaviour, even throwing in a little Biblical business – 'Do unto others as you wish to be done to you' – in an attempt to bring the culprits to book.

Where the gloves come off, lines such as 'Slaughter when you feast/You disrespect the beast/Make our beds and lie there, take our share' make their point with eloquent vehemence. However, the halfhearted arrangement makes 'Waste Not Want Not' an opportunity squandered, too laid-back and diffident for the subject's requisite gravity.

'Day After Day' 3.47 (Hynde/Honeyman-Scott)
Pretenders II's ninth track could have been perfectly at home as the second or third on *Pretenders*. It even evokes Lake Erie, the sea-sized expanse whose brisk winds blow crime and tumbleweeds down the post-industrial main streets of Cleveland and Akron. The song might be about yearning and loneliness, but Hynde's words are even harder to crack open than usual. Lines such as 'war is waging endlessly' allied to the aforesaid Great Lake recall Chrissie's Ohio youth, a period during which kids were shot down at Kent State and Vietnam hovered, ominous as a locked and loaded Chinook. Yet when she sings winsomely of the song's subject travelling 'over somebody's winter this afternoon', she seems lonely and aching, perhaps for a lover from a youth now lost forever to the swirling, impenetrable mists of rock 'n' roll success. For celebrity, weathering this city to the next, one stoned dash after another between tour bus, gig and afterparty, makes demands like few others on young, untested psyches.

Musically there's no grey area, as Jimmy lets loose a broadside of eighth notes and assembles as few chords as he needs to hammer home this small but perfectly formed slab of classic guitar rock. For a quietly-promoted single that reached only number 45 on the UK chart (107 in Australia, the only other territorial release), 'Day After Day' was twinned with the Martin Chambers-penned 'In The Sticks': a sparky instrumental that sounds like a 1963 Jet Harris & Tony Meehan B-side, complete with a short drum solo from Martin of which ex-Shadow Tony would surely have been proud.

'Jealous Dogs' 5.37 (Hynde)
Critically negative reactions in some quarters to *Pretenders II* suggested that kickback against The Pretenders' success had become a national sport, particularly among the hacks for whom the band once had been the next best thing, until they weren't. Only relatively recently, Chrissie Hynde had acquired the first-magnitude stardom she claimed not to have pursued back in 1978. But for a woman whose natural instinct was to retreat into her private redoubt accompanied by a flurry of well-judged pungency (paradoxically, given the call to rock 'n' roll inevitably makes very public property of the most retiring), being a poster child for the vicarious and a vessel for fandom's hopes and fears must have been far from easy.

In its broadest sense, 'Jealous Dogs' is a platform from which Chrissie takes potshots at the politics of envy, perhaps specifically women she believes might have designs on her man of the time. Yet there's another, even tighter, element of jealousy at play. This relates to her recently forged kinship with the already-married Ray Davies, a liaison that proved so dangerous that a furious Mrs Davies called in her lawyers. In the ensuing suit, Ray's second wife's advisors charmlessly named Chrissie Hynde as 'an adultress'. This could have been a mistake with substantial, if nuanced, legal implications, since *Britannica* defines the damning noun as a *married* woman who has sex with a man who is not her husband. I would put it to m'learned friends that this appears to be a *prima facie* case of attorney-concocted cockup, Chrissie being single before and throughout the four years she and Ray were getting it on.

This hussy (alleged) might have been tempted to brief legal eagles pursuant to an action of her own. But Chrissie would have been no songwriter at all if she'd allowed the situation to escape her pen. While it's tempting to identify Ray's other half as the plaintiff (even though the adultress jibe is probably innocent, if unedifying, legalese thrown in by over-exuberant lawyers keen to do right by their client), poetic ambiguities abound. Chrissie lets loose both barrels, the Hyndeian vitriol 100% concentrated:

> Those jealous dogs, always on the alert
> Tattle tale rights
> They'll take your back and leave your shirt

Above: Led by Chrissie Hynde, one of the greatest stars of her generation, The Pretenders perfectly balanced punk, pop and mainstream rock. (*Alamy*)

Left: Few debuts have surpassed 1980's *Pretenders*: good looks, great hair, an instinctive grasp of rock's rebel ethos. (*Sire*)

Right: Three floor-filling minutes, with extra swaggering groove and a side order of sass: 1979's 'Brass In Pocket' was a worldwide hit. (*Sire*)

Left: The sleeve of 'Precious', released as a single in The Netherlands; like many others, the song evoked Chrissie's teen years in Cleveland. (*Sire*)

Right: 'Message Of Love' was a British number 11 in February 1981: 'We're social creatures', Chrissie said. 'We have to look after each other.' (*Sire*)

Left: *Extended Play* reworked an old concept: just five tracks, but the 12" vinyl format left many scratching their heads. (*Sire*)

Right: *Pretenders II*: the cover didn't spoil a superb second album. From left to right: Chrissie Hynde, James Honeyman-Scott, Martin Chambers, Pete Farndon. (*Sire*)

Left: Christine Ellen Hynde's peachy Firestone High Yearbook photo. London and The Pretenders were ahead. Who knew?

Right: The Telecaster! The Marshall stack! The attitude! Born to perform, Chrissie had rock 'n' roll coming out of her ears. (*Heather Harris*)

Left: Chrissie captured in concert with The Pretenders at London's Lyceum Theatre in 1981. (*Getty*)

Right: The original Pretenders in 1979, looking moody and trying to give up smoking. From left to right: Pete, Martin, Chrissie, Jimmy. (*Getty*)

Left: The Pretenders' first lead guitarist, James Honeyman-Scott: a gifted axeman who would influence many players to come.

Right: The original Pretenders: a promo shot for 'Talk Of The Town' in 1981. From left to right: Pete, Martin, Chrissie, Jimmy. (*Simon Fowler*)

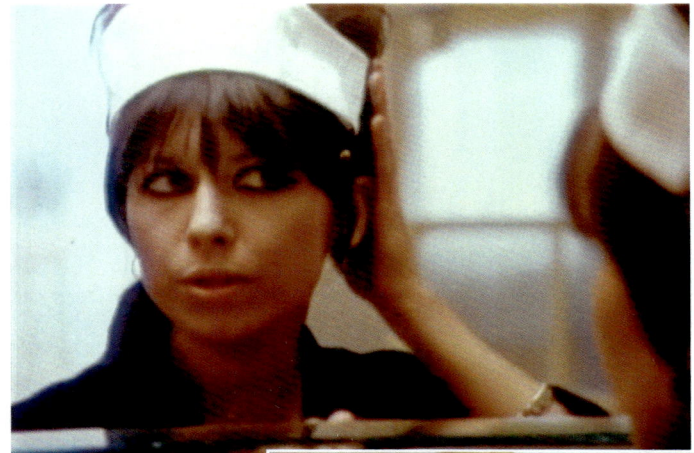

Left: Chrissie, a coquettish Midwest waitress transplanted to North Kensington: a still from the 'Brass In Pocket' promo video.

Right: 'I'm special, so special, gotta have some of your attention…' Jimmy hopefully places his order in the 'Brass In Pocket' music video.

Left: Jimmy and Chrissie trading licks in 1981, around the time of *Pretenders II*.

Right: Martin and Pete in 1981.

Left: Chrissie Hynde, from the 'Talk Of The Town' video in 1980; encouraging and empowering women to front rock 'n' roll bands.

Right: The Pretenders in 1980; the op-art set for the promo video helped push 'Talk Of The Town' to number eight in the UK.

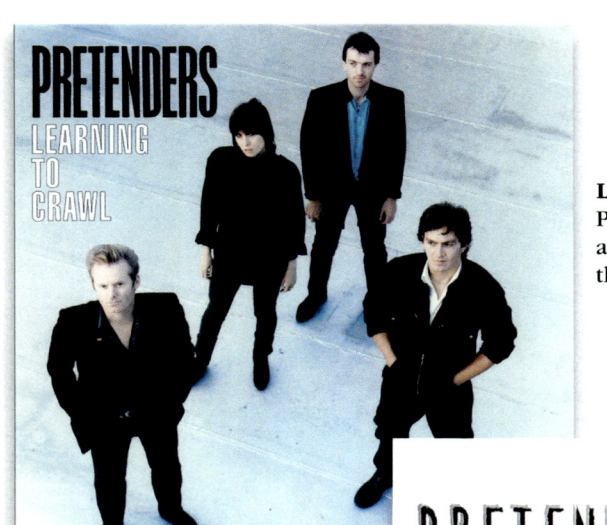

Left: *Learning To Crawl*: The Pretenders dusted off, picked up and started over with a stunning third album. (*Sire*)

Right: A number-17 UK hit and number-five hit on *Billboard*'s Hot 100 in 1982, 'Back On The Chain Gang' was written by Chrissie in memory of Jimmy. (*Sire*)

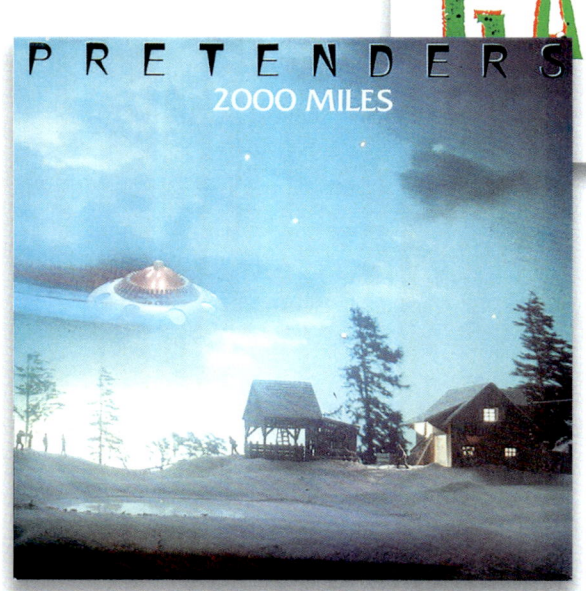

Left: As exhilarating and diffuse as condensed breath on a crisp, cold winter's morning, '2000 Miles' was a festive UK number 15 in 1983. (*Sire*)

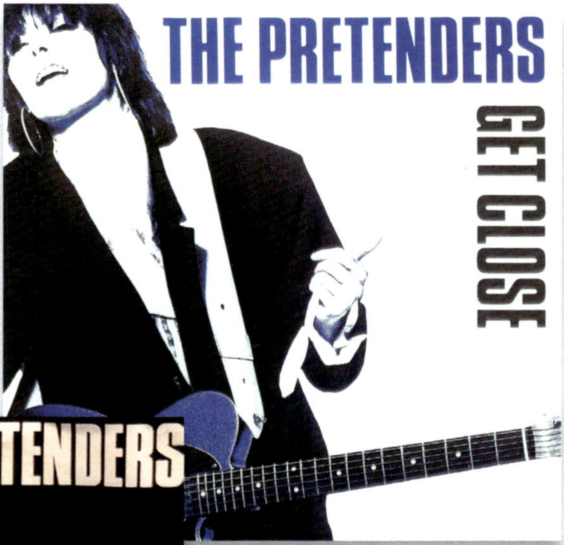

Right: *Get Close*: the fourth album's big shoulders carried the forms and feelings of the mid-1980s in a sea-change for The Pretenders. (*Sire*)

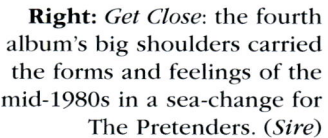

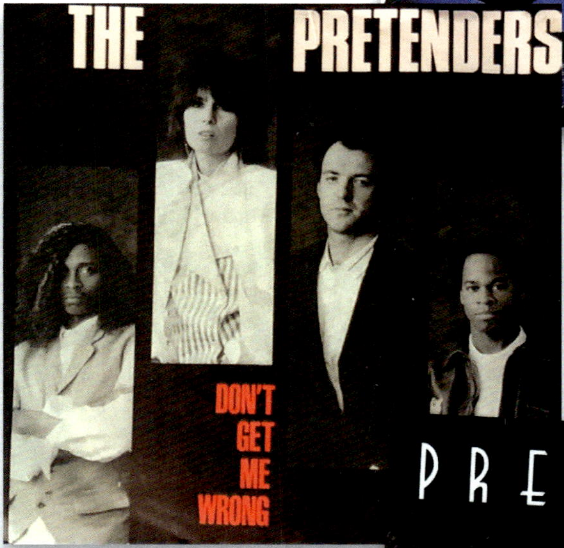

Left: The *Get Close* band and the sleeve of the 'Don't Get Me Wrong' single. From left to right: T. M. Stevens, Chrissie, Robbie McIntosh, Blair Cunningham. (*Sire*)

Right: Shinily professional, the fifth album proved a grower, creeping up on the listener before anyone realised it. (*Sire*)

Left: Original Pretender Martin Chambers: a revolving-door relationship – Chrissie would return to the drummer again and again.

Below: The Pretenders circa *Learning To Crawl*. From left to right: Malcolm Foster, Martin, Chrissie, Robbie McIntosh. (*Ron Wolfson/WireImage*)

Above: Chrissie and Robbie in 1984: the ideal angle of incidence of a mid-slung Telecaster – not to mention a Les Paul. (*Getty*)

Left: Mr and Mrs Jim Kerr in Central Park, NYC, on their wedding day, 5 May 1984. Out of shot: the horse-drawn carriage. (*Alamy*)

Left: Chrissie joins the Salvation Army for the '2000 Miles' promo video.

Right: It was this big, Santa, honest. Chrissie Hynde and festive friends in the promo video for '2000 Miles'.

Left: Digging the promo video for 'Back On The Chain Gang', directed by Chrissie's old friend and landlord Don Letts.

Right: Chrissie framed nicely by Don Letts for the 'Back On The Chain Gang' music video.

Left: The promo video for 'Don't Get Me Wrong' was a homage to the cult British TV show *The Avengers*, with Chrissie playing the legendary Emma Peel.

Right: Chrissie as Mrs Peel in a deerstalker, searching for John Steed in the 'Don't Get Me Wrong' *Avengers* video. Steed (Patrick Macnee) even had a cameo.

Left: T. M. 'Shaka Zulu' Stevens: skin in the game with Miles Davis and Mahavishnu, the bassist brought agile, liquid chops to *Get Close*.

Right: Bernie Worrell: one of the most experienced sessioneers to play with The Pretenders. (*Boston Music Photography*)

Left: Ex-Detroit Emeralds, Denise La Salle and Haircut One Hundred drummer Blair Cunningham replaced Martin Chambers for *Get Close* and *Packed!*.

Right: Malcolm Foster: the bassist came in for Pete, then walked following Martin's dismissal. Later, he played sessions for Chrissie's ex in Simple Minds.

Left: Chrissie's former squeeze, *NME* journalist and one of rock's most celebrated gonzo writers, Nick Kent.

Right: Chrissie with Ray Davies, co-founding genius of The Kinks, writer of 'Stop Your Sobbing' and The Great Pretender's beau for four tempestuous years. (*Robert Matheu*)

Above: Chrissie, flanked by Natalie (left) and Yasmin (right). Both daughters inherited their mother's sense of mischief. (*Richard Young/Startraks Photo*)

Below: Large chicken to go: Chrissie and feathered friend take on the fast-food industry. (*Getty*)

> Like that jealous bitch
> Always wanting more
> The courts have made her rich
> And the click of high heels down the corridor
> Jealous, jealous, jealous dogs.

'That jealous bitch' in the first verse may be an ironic self-reference. Is this how Chrissie suggests she is seen by some of the hangers-on with whom she's forced to treat: the paparazzi, or the often fickle, sycophantic commentators who sit in judgment? This being the case, and those being (at the time) male-dominated professions, the song seems to be waving a flag and a fist for womankind, despite her historic disapproval of such posturing.

Whoever the wretched target, 'Jealous Dogs' is a deep-cut gem. Moody and bass-driven under Jimmy's silvery guitar, all battered into submission by Martin's clumping 4/4, it's as if 'Mystery Achievement' has been slowed down, its inexorable advance reimagined as a martially sinister soundtrack to a (decent) remake of *Rollerball*.

'The English Roses' 4.30 (Hynde)

The firebreathing virago of 'Bad Boys Get Spanked' or 'Pack It Up' isn't the most obvious bedfellow for the subject of the penultimate song on *Pretenders II*:

> Fruit cut from the vine
> Forgot and left to rot
> Long before its time
> This is a story
> About the girl who lived next door
> Looking for someone to hold.

Another unsung jewel on an album whose treasures are leisurely in the reveal but rich in the appreciation, 'The English Roses' is a masterly, late-Beatley vignette of solitude, a touching depiction of a lonely young woman left high and dry by life almost before it's begun. Chrissie describes someone who is resigned to rejection, eternally disappointed by 'a thousand broken dates'. A rose pressed into the pages of a hymnal and 'fruit cut from the vine' (paraphrasing John 15:2) hint at a personal religiosity more mainstream, perhaps, than the Vaishnavism Chrissie will soon embrace. In the last of *Pretenders II*'s smart little character studies, the writer shows her willingness and ability to move on from the vitriolic aggression of her earliest efforts. Never a willing evangelist – at least not until her vegetarianism turns radical – she's now happy as a writer to let a belief system filter gently through a lyric, rather than to box the ears of the listener.

As for the song's subject, the jilted one has been interpreted as an ugly duckling who can't find a man. This is a harsh, reductionist view. There are more complex reasons for her melancholy than the merely physical, and it is unlikely that Chrissie Hynde would paint a picture so heartless and lacking in nuance of someone clearly ill-equipped to answer back. This is evidence of the fast-gathering maturity of Hynde's songwriting, now sitting beside an actorly facility for inhabiting, with empathy and compassion, a character who may not be her own. There's no notion of autobiography, even though, as has been seen, Chrissie is far more vulnerable and sensitive than her hardass mien would suggest. It could even be said that, if this is evidence of a talent for impartial portraiture of the lonely and isolated – an exacting task for any wordsmith to pull off – Chrissie Hynde is now writing as convincingly as any acknowledged master of the craft, from Paul McCartney ('Eleanor Rigby') to Keith Richards ('Ruby Tuesday'), from David Bowie ('Space Oddity') to Jimmy Webb ('Wichita Lineman').

'The English Roses' creeps up from behind. Allowed the airplay to settle into recognition, the simple but delicious gearshifts within the unassuming arrangement feel like old friends – hence the Beatle comparison – and Jimmy Scott's guitar is a restrained joy throughout. The song is one-paced and its dynamics are modest, but this plays to its favour; the quiet change at 1.43 is so subtly gorgeous that anything more involved would bury it.

'Louie Louie' 3.29 (Hynde)

If a descendant melancholia has typified the second side of *Pretenders II*, the mood is lifted by an exuberant finale. Without hearing it, given Chrissie's exaltation of Ray Davies and all his works, it's natural to assume 'Louie Louie' is the old Richard Berry three-chord boilerplate, already interpreted in varying states of respect, decay and affectionate lampoonery by everyone from The Kingsmen to The Kinks to Frank Zappa. With its horn section and Jimmy's squeaky Farfisa, this loses a chord and merely *sounds* as if it could have been part of Murray the K's AM playlist 15 years earlier. Trumpeter Henry Lowther and tenorist Chris Mercer were old-sweat jazzers, session men and graduates of the John Mayall finishing school for the blues; it's unlikely they and second trumpet Jim Wilson needed much prompting, from either band or producer, to let rip like Mitch Ryder in the Peppermint Lounge in 1965.

Everyone's having a whale of a time, Pete and Martin erecting a fast, uncrackable rhythm, the horns pummelling furiously. At 1.20, coaxed by Chrissie's rousing hey hey heys, Jimmy slips on the bottleneck for a thrilling slide solo, and there's a great bridge at 1.45, as everyone briefly lets up – all save a stabbed, one-note rhythm guitar and poor Martin slaving over a snare drum that's by now considering assault charges – for Chrissie's enigmatic, stream-of-consciousness words, cooed in upper register by the band and answered by the singer herself:

(Ooh, pattycake, I love your daughter, I wanna take now
Ooh, pattycake, I love your daughter, I wanna take)
You move so fine, yeah, what a scene I said
Mmm, kinda aquiline, yeah, baby, saw through this now.

The song's oblique references to Road Spiders and Supergliders suggest she once again has the Heavy Bikers in mind. The words spew from her lips like liquid fire, apparently adlibbed and the perfect lyrical foil to the supertight but uninhibited arrangement. Like the first album's 'Mystery Achievement' – which bass-centric frenzy 'Louie Louie' superficially echoes – it's a barn-burning finale, upbeat and optimistic, with little evidence of the hopped-up weariness that was eating so damagingly into The Pretenders as they approached the most cataclysmic period of their short existence.

'Louie Louie' was released as a single in the US only, where it peaked at number 110 on *Billboard*.

Associated
Live At The Santa Monica Civic 1981
Promo only, first released in 1982; bonus CD with 2006 reissue of Pretenders II
'The Wait'/'The Adultress'/'Message Of Love'/'Louie Louie'/'Talk Of The Town'/'Birds Of Paradise'/'Up The Neck'/'Bad Boys Get Spanked'/'Stop Your Sobbing'/'Private Life'/'Kid'/'Day After Day'/'(Your Love Keeps Lifting Me) Higher And Higher'
A good state-of-the-union address from The Pretenders' 93-show US tour in 1981. Following what's virtually a greatest-hits set, the band finish with a frisky version of 'Higher And Higher', the dance classic by Jackie Wilson – Chrissie's first 'squeeze' – accompanied by touring buddies the Bureau, an English brass-soul group formed from an early-doors Dexys Midnight Runners.

The Pretenders ... *On Track*

Learning To Crawl (1984)

Personnel
Chrissie Hynde: guitars, vocals
Martin Chambers: drums, vocals
Robbie McIntosh: lead guitar, vocals
Malcolm Foster: bass, vocals
Billy Bremner: lead guitar ('Back On The Chain Gang', 'My City Was Gone'); rhythm guitar, vocals ('Thin Line Between Love And Hate')
Tony Butler: bass ('Back On The Chain Gang', 'My City Was Gone')
Andrew Bodner: bass, vocals ('Thin Line Between Love And Hate')
Paul Carrack: piano, vocals ('Thin Line Between Love And Hate')
Produced at Air Studios, London, by Chris Thomas
Engineers: Steve Churchyard, Jeremy Allom
Released: January 1984
Highest chart position: UK: 11, US: 5

> I kept the thing alive very much in the spirit of the music because I didn't want to let it go out of respect for Pete and Jimmy. I wasn't prepared to not play those songs anymore.
> Chrissie Hynde, Swedish TV, 2015

> I roll with the punches in my life. I don't get traumatised.
> Chrissie Hynde, *The Blue Railroad*, 2011

By 1983, The Pretenders were in credit by two albums and numerous globally successful singles. In the world outside, the gritty, analogue authenticity of the band's punk midwives was a distant memory. From the late 1970s, popular culture had been bossed by the Blitz kids: the heirs to the cult of the new romantics were androgynous, post-Numan humanoids with digital keyboards and identikit floppy haircuts, their music sometimes so coldly detached it could have been incubated by moonlighting neurosurgeons. There was still some good news: excellent, electrocentric pop bands such as Depeche Mode, Soft Cell, OMD and Human League were well across the new technology, owning the era much as Elvis, the Fabs, The Stones, Motown, Stax, ABBA and the Pistols had, respectively, theirs. But too many fellow travellers, wedded to binary code, were diluting the newer music. Suddenly the dancefloor took on the sterility of a cleanroom, so ubiquitous were the processed percussion and chilly, dismembered synths.

This was the world into which a third album was lobbed by The Pretenders: looking hard, staying relevant and refining what they already knew, cocking a Hyndeian snook at what was expected of them – even as their world caved in.

At their alley-cat best, The Pretenders left dirt under your fingernails then cleaned them out with a switchblade. To their credit, and against the odds, the band were able to keep the rebel faith into their third album. It's as if they knew that introducing synthesisers and syndrums would be like fitting stabiliser wheels to a racing bike: they'd stop you falling over, but at the expense of the velocity and cliff-edge thrills, even the occasional scar-tissue, so crucial to proper rock 'n' roll.

Sometimes, however, the sense of danger could boil over from the comfortably abstract to the all-too-horribly real. In London on 14 June 1982, barely weeks after hastily marrying Conover Kennard, an American model he'd met in Tokyo, Pete Farndon was sacked from The Pretenders. Manager Dave Hill, who wielded the knife, offered the age-old political canards: musical differences, new beginnings and whatnot. The reality was that time finally had to be called on the band's exposure to Pete's ruinous drug habit. Supported by Martin Chambers, James Honeyman-Scott had already read the riot act: it was him or me. Worse was to come.

Two days in from Pete's dismissal, after attending a benefit show for MS-afflicted Ronnie Lane, Jimmy fell to a fatal heart attack, believed due to an overdose of cocaine aggravated by a line of heroin. With dreadful irony, the guitarist had taken the latter to help him sleep. Although he'd been using amphetamines for years before joining The Pretenders and his drug-related mood swings could be as alienating as Pete's, Jimmy's addictions were never quite as dark as his bandmate's. Opiates, however, are heartless creditors; whether the user is carefree party animal or shooting gallery wreck, its interest rates are as prohibitively high.

By April 1983, Pete was in the throes of forming a new band. To be called Samurai (after the clothes the bassist frequently modelled onstage, toggling with the biker jackets), it would comprise guitarist Henry Padovani, organist Mick Gallagher, singer Steve Allen and, perhaps ill-advisedly, drummer Topper Headon. (Equally ill-omened, if for different reasons, was the liaison briefly tabled between Farndon and Nick Kent.) Topper had been evicted from behind The Clash's traps for similarly junk-related violations. But while he survived, eventually becoming a charity worker and tireless advocate for sobriety, on 14 April Pete mainlined a fatal speedball of cocaine and heroin. Conover found him in the bath in which he probably drowned, despite the coroner's finding of a drug overdose. In the last he'd gone full-monty rocker, for whom image was everything – living fast, dying young, yet another victim of a destructively addictive belief in the lifestyle's transcendence. As Chrissie told *Rolling Stone*, 'He would see a picture of himself in the paper, and he thought that was him. But it wasn't; it was just a photograph.' Given the pair's history, Pete's downfall must have been like losing a limb.

Three months before Pete died, Chrissie Hynde and Pete's romantic successor Ray Davies introduced the world to their first and only child, Natalie Rae Hynde (as an imminently post-Ray, vaguely post-feminist statement, Chrissie registered the baby's surname as her own). If the infant's postpartum attempts at mobility provided her mother with a usefully *pret-a-porter* title for The Pretenders' third album, it was one freighted with a double-entendre that, with Pete's passing, would feel doubly unhappy. It was always tempting to see *Learning To Crawl* as an allusion to how, in their agonies, the band vowed to dust off, pick up and start over. From the viewpoint of most Pretenders fans, the title felt like a positioning statement, assuring the world that Chrissie Hynde and Martin Chambers not only refused to be cowed by Jimmy's loss, but would doggedly soldier on despite the second tragedy ten months later. Although by then Pete was no longer officially a Pretender – ex or not, he was always part of the family – his passing marked the end of the band in their purest incarnation. Had the bassist gotten clean and been able to stay or return, had Jimmy not fallen to the rock 'n' roll disease (and who knows to what extent his friend's mental and physical collapse contributed to the guitarist's own dark passion?), The Pretenders in their pomp might have gone on to still greater glory. What force they remained would be highly successful but inconsistent, fragmented and occasionally a little too polished for the once rough and ready rockers. Posterity would teach that the band did not better the first trio of albums; many even aver they never surpassed *Pretenders*. Memories of what the two fellow founding members had brought to the all-too-brief party, of how the original quartet oozed proper rock 'n' roll in all its denim-&-leather defiance as effectively as any of their peers: these issues were surely at the forefront of Chrissie's thoughts and creative processes as she contemplated the future.

Losing two key players from a young quartet that now bestrode the world was an earthquake seismic enough to deck artists less resilient than Chrissie and Martin. So it's to the surviving members' credit that the album worked as well as it did. Given the preceding convulsions, *Learning To Crawl* is arguably The Pretenders' most historically important record. The band weren't so much learning to crawl, as reasserting the proud swagger that had defined them since 1978.

Following Jimmy's death, Chrissie and Martin assembled a provisional group with guitarist Billy Bremner, late of Scotty favourite Dave Edmunds' Rockpile, and Tony Butler, bassist with Big Country. Completed by Robbie McIntosh on rhythm guitar, that lineup played on the single 'Back On The Chain Gang' b/w 'My City Was Gone', released in September 1982, both songs destined for the new album. Bremner contributed to another track and the next single, 'Thin Line Between Love And Hate', for which Butler was replaced by Andrew Bodnar (bass player with Graham Parker & The Rumour) while ex-Ace, Squeeze and Roxy Music keyboardist Paul Carrack filled in on piano.

Despite a lurking fluidity of Pretenders personnel, solid order was returned for the rest of the album. McIntosh, a 26-year-old classically-trained guitarist from Sutton in Surrey, had racked up an enviable scorecard of sessions for such stars as Kevin Ayers, Joe Cocker and Roger Daltrey. In June 1982, Jimmy Scott – with another savage irony, just one day before he died – asked Robbie, an acquaintance since 1977, to join The Pretenders. (Jimmy was more thoughtful and far-sighted than his speed-fried, stoned-Tigger nonchalance ever suggested; undoubtedly a fine musical director in the making, the guitarist looked to fatten the band's sound onstage, as well as explore the avenues that might be opened with additional musicians.) After a respectful pause, Robbie answered the call in December 1982, bringing in bassist Malcolm Foster, with whom he'd spent five years playing in numerous live and studio settings. The pair had developed a rapport that entirely suited their new gig: an established band for which empathy, both musical and emotional, was mother's milk. With the four-piece equilibrium restored, November 1983 saw the single release of '2000 Miles', a Christmas hit and later a hardy perennial for the supermarket festive compilation album.

The reinvigorated band showed admirable resolve in bringing the new album to fruition. But as Chrissie told James Henke of *Rolling Stone* in 1984, 'It wasn't exactly a barrel of monkeys.' Martin said of one studio session, 'Tony Butler was playing a bass line, and Chrissie walked in and said, 'What's that?' She didn't even know it was 'Private Life' and she wrote the bloody song! That's the sort of state she was in.' Chrissie told of periods of irrationally emotional resentment towards the others: 'The first time I saw one of them – I think it was Malcolm – walk in with a Pretenders t-shirt on, I thought, who is he to be wearing a Pretenders shirt?'

Chrissie awarded herself maternity leave before and after Natalie's arrival, so *Learning To Crawl* was almost a year in gestation. And while its quality salutes the tenacity of Chrissie and Martin in the face of near-extinction, respect is surely also due Chris Thomas, whose third innings as The Pretenders' producer helped realise a suite of songs that was much better than it perhaps had any right to be.

As discussed, the band were not tempted to pasteurise their music with the otherwise all-pervasive Big Tech – that would come later. *Learning To Crawl* was, at heart, a great rock 'n' roll album, retaining the sway and arrogance of youth and with nary synth nor electronic tam-tam in sight. However, Thomas was nothing if not an astute and judicious reader of the moment. He was happy to adapt whatever technology was available as a means to an end, such as plumping up Martin's already voluptuous percussion while stopping short of what Elvis Costello would one day colourfully critique as 'that 1980s fascist drum sound'. As *Learning To Crawl*'s engineer, Steve Churchyard recounted in 2005 to online magazine *Sound On Sound*:

> The live tracking, playing with the Linn drum, putting it out through the PA … Chris ensured that it sounded very organic while at the same time employing some trickery that the listener wouldn't really be aware of in order to make it sound exciting … we might just set up a mic in the middle that would have some kind of ridiculous compression on it, and mix that back in there. This was the result of Chris having been George Martin's assistant on *The Beatles* through the Badfinger days and working with Roxy Music and Brian Eno. He's been around a lot of creative people.

Having learned well at the feet of the future Sir George, Chris now rose to his third Pretenders brief as to the manner born. Churchyard told of how the producer's understanding of the band's best self now entitled him to a cheesy but inevitable sobriquet:

> Without a doubt, if George Martin was the fifth Beatle, then Chris Thomas was the fifth Pretender. He was hands-on in all aspects of the recording, whereas a lot of producers produce from their phones in the car. He was there for every moment of whatever was going on, directing either me or the musicians.

The perceptive journalist Kurt Loder spotted the production nous and nuance Thomas deployed in order to raise a coherent record from The Pretenders' emotional fallout and fragmented, often disparate, human resources: '*Learning To Crawl*, at the very least, achieves a professional rebirth that seemed uncertain as recently as a few months ago', Loder wrote in his February 1984 review for *Rolling Stone*:

> Instrumentally, the band has its moments, but the late Honeyman-Scott's latticework lyricism is often missed and probably irreplaceable. There's also an occasional unevenness to the overall band sound – outside musicians were brought in to play on certain tracks before new bassist Malcolm Foster and guitarist Robbie McIntosh signed aboard – but producer Chris Thomas, for the most part, manages to pull things together.

The New York Times was glad that the album 'kicks and churns and growls without a hint of politeness', while Mark Deming at *Allmusic* would later pay tribute to how effectively Chrissie had forged a new start: '[She] pulled it off with a striking mixture of courage, strength and great rock 'n' roll; with the exception of the instant-classic debut album, it's The Pretenders' finest work.'

For the sleeve, Paul Cox captures the quartet as extras from *Black Hawk Down*: Delta Force grunts, uniformed in suitably funereal black, on a neutral tarmac seen from a descending gunship. Chrissie is on heightened alert; her expression hints at enemy action by the photographer, like Churchill after Karsh swiped away the great man's cigar. On the back, someone shot by Alyssa Cooper but decapitated by the sleeve designer – probably McIntosh, judging by the guitarist's then-favoured Astrakhan collar – strums a Stratocaster. Among the dustjacket montage of individual band members onstage, Malcolm's pose with his P-bass is remarkably Pete-like, while Chrissie apparently flips the bird at her audience.

Critics aside, *Learning To Crawl* was acclaimed by record buyers, making number 11 on the UK albums chart and peaking on the *Billboard* 200 at number five: The Pretenders' best album performance in the US.

'Middle Of The Road' 4.16 (Hynde)

Martin's blappa-blappa intro is eloquent confirmation: The Pretenders have no plans to be cowed, either by a changing musical landscape or by personal tragedies and the tetchy responses of media and the music business. Neither are the band obviously bound for the eponymous centre, although Chrissie Hynde's own position is less clear-cut.

By the album's release, Chrissie had turned 32, middle-aged in rock 'n' roll terms and a factor in her transitioning from the embers of her cherished original group. But if the middle of the road is a place tenanted as much by genuine talent that shouldn't be there as by slight ephemera that can be nowhere else (Suzi Quatro, among others, wobbled uncertainly between the two), the first track on *Learning To Crawl* locates The Pretenders far from it.

Ever counter-intuitive, in 2014 Chrissie assured the *Austin American Statesman* the way of the Tao was, in essence, the path she'd always trod. She told Wes Eichenwald:

> My personal discipline has been to try to stay in the middle, always, no matter what I'm doing. If I buy a jacket and it comes in three sizes, I want a medium. You have to learn how to temper yourself and hold back till you get to the end.

Chrissie was hardly the first 63-year-old with a hinterland of hellraising to make such a declaration. She likened her temperate middle-aged self to the shrill who took on both the Memphis PD and Lemmy Kilmister (although as already mentioned, despite the occasional lapse, her instinctive default position was semi-detached from the obligatory misbehaviour of rock 'n' rollers, not least her sadly departed bandmates). But biology and rock's baked-in entropy wait for no-one; by 1983, The Pretenders were approaching that moment in a successful group's lifecycle when safety beckons. The recording industry can be unforgiving, as persuasive as Nurse Ratched on a bad-hair day, rarely sympathetic to art except when dangling percentages and a stadium tour of North America. (Many surrender: early on, Simple Minds fashioned post-punk into an icily synth-laden European tundra; their music, not to mention Jim Kerr's pudding-basin haircut, was among the era's most fascinating. By the time of 'Don't You (Forget About Me)' and *The Breakfast Club*, they'd given in to hair gel, pop-star smiles and sound checks at the enormodrome.)

Thankfully (for now), Chrissie is having none of it. Instead, she does what we've all hoped for but haven't dared to expect. Her middle of the road is a duality, positive and negative – yin and yang, since we're in Tao territory. The first verse finds her pugnaciously standing four-square 'in the middle of life with my plans behind me'. Though she has a smile for everyone, she must be allowed to go her own way. 'In the middle of the road, you see the darndest things', she observes in the second, as she proceeds to excoriate the global rich who exploit children in 'the bloody third world'. Yet, she – happily? – inhabits the middle herself, resigned to her age but content with her burgeoning faith and the joyous challenges of raising a child from whose father she's about to become estranged. By the end, she seems jaded, 'not the cat I used to be', going home and tired as hell. The messages are mixed, as if setting a borderline future against a past whose promise, once so assured, has been so savagely dashed.

More certain is the arrangement, hard as 4/4 fuck, a rocking carapace welded to earworm memorability. Despite the general absence of melody, the result is still classic Pretenders: the punk confederates who've long discovered the knack of releasing every hard rocker's inner pop fan. Robbie McIntosh's brilliant rock 'n' roll guitar proves Chrissie's faith was well placed – as, bless him, was Jimmy's – while towards the end the boss even takes up gob-iron and spits out a tooth-grinding harmonica solo that wouldn't have disgraced an early Stones record.

Chrissie would later dismiss 'Middle Of The Road' as 'a total Stones rip-off', but it's easily one of the band's best performances, the single (the third from *Learning To Crawl*) mysteriously beaching in the UK at 87. In America, *Billboard* allowed no further than number 19, although the mainstream US rock chart showed better taste and placed it at number two.

'Back On The Chain Gang' 3.51 (Hynde)
Chrissie recalled how, during The Pretenders' infancy, she would part-bake songs then bring them to the band, whereupon Jimmy Honeyman-Scott would 'add the hooks and make them into something great'. The late guitarist was front and centre of Chrissie's thoughts when she wrote the album's second track, already a hit single on its original release three months after Jimmy died and destined for the soundtrack to *The King Of Comedy* in March 1983. Recorded while Chrissie was three months pregnant with Natalie, 'Back On The Chain Gang' mines a similar seam to the album's first cut. Written in Jimmy's memory, the song touches upon how the aloof treadmill of the record business ignores grief and other human emotions, imposing on sometimes naive stars the buttoned-up, business-as-usual *froideur* normally associated with bodies less sympathetic to the rock 'n' roll dream.

Chrissie's 'chain gang' isn't dissimilar to her ambiguous 'middle': an amorphous blob of business managers, A&Rs, hacks and record company CEOs, all desperate to exact feudal tribute and control. Much as she wishes they'd butt out and permit her to grieve Jimmy in her own time – she wrote and recorded the song shortly after the guitarist's passing, but several months before Pete's – 'the powers that be that force us to live like we do' are anxious to pull her back into a manageable orbit, thereby governing the forward momentum of both her and that capaciously generous piggy bank known as The Pretenders.

It's said that 'the picture of you' – used twice in the lyric, in a delicately visual, even cinematographic evocation of reflective longing – was of Ray

Davies, the photo fished from her wallet as she sadly contemplated writing in remembrance of Jimmy. This works, of course; why would Chrissie not conflate, even subconsciously, her partner and the father of her child with a deceased bandmate she'd come to love so dearly? Memories are released, good and bad, then projected from one individual to another. She has lost Jimmy and may be parting soon from Ray. That Chrissie should feel an equally free-flowing wellspring of hurt for both, expressing it so beautifully yet without a jot of maudlin sentimentality, is extraordinarily affecting.

'Back On The Chain Gang' started life as a passing fancy during soundchecks for the band's most recent US tour. 'When [Jimmy] died, I finished the song thinking about him,' Chrissie said later. 'When we went in to record it, we got Billy Bremner to play on it.' Steve Churchyard talked of Chrissie's single-mindedness in getting her vocals down in the studio. For 'Back On The Chain Gang', the singer refused to share the control room even with her closest comrades, who were exiled upstairs to play pool:

> Only Chris Thomas and myself were in the room while Chrissie sang, and he'd have to coax a performance out of her … On the surface, Chrissie was all business when it came to ['Back On The Chain Gang']; let's get this done, and don't let anybody in the control room or else you'll suffer the wrath of Chrissie. If she was at all acerbic, then rightly so. The studio is never a very natural environment in which to sing, so we'd do anything we could to make her comfortable. If you catch her on the wrong day, things can be heavy, but she can also be very funny, and she was very easy to work with when we did 'Chain Gang'. Only later did I realise how emotional it must have been for her.

Churchyard had nothing but praise for Bremner's single-take, Nashville-tinged solo:

> I think he just played it. I don't remember any struggle. It was one of those inspired things. Everyone flipped at how he played it and then we all went down the pub.

'Back On The Chain Gang' was The Pretenders' most successful American hit single, making number five on *Billboard*'s Hot 100 and number four on its Rock Top Tracks. It peaked at number 17 in the UK. Its legacy endures: Bruce Springsteen, Morrissey and The Bangles are among the stars to have covered the song.

'Time The Avenger' 4.56 (Hynde)
Interrogating the idea of complacent fat cats 'with [their] girls and desk and leather chair' is fast becoming a minor theme of *Learning To Crawl*. Like so many, this one thinks time is his friend. He installs a mistress, his 'perfect

stranger'. Yet in his hubris, he fails to foresee the consequences once Mother Nature has exercised her uncanny knack of redressing a balance: of levelling ground that has been fissured by arrogance. When the passing of time etches weariness into the face of his lover as irreversibly as it does the family he's betrayed, he's bereft, high and dry, with only the booze to deaden the pain.

Chrissie reminds the beancounters that, no matter the trimmings and trappings of business success, time is finite, forever an implacable enemy. It marches on – of course it does – and will never, in the end, tolerate decency and kindness being bent out of shape by power and self-aggrandisement. It's naïve to imagine such a perfect world, where natural justice prevails and love conquers all. Here Chrissie's growing philosophical idealism (ushered in, to some extent, by loss) once more gains elegant expression, denouncing a pitiless decade in which conspicuous consumption is fast forming its own religion.

'Time The Avenger' has a 1960s club flavour, once again channelling Spencer Davis (this time 'Keep On Running'). The band set up a nicely urgent vamp, over which Chrissie issues her critique as a typically rapid-fire semi-rap.

'Watching The Clothes' 2.53 (Hynde)
More from the 1960s: a crisp slice of proletarian social commentary, fixing Phil Ochs to Chuck Berry as explained by the Swinging Blue Jeans. Chrissie adopts the persona of her careworn cocktail waitress, except that the prosecution of her menial duties – kissin' ass in the diner, serving sour cream with the potato – is a long way from saving the cash to see The MC5 at the Grande Ballroom, but is actually, hey, about making ends meet. Her social conscience demands that she scrutinises who benefits from her serfdom. Their identification as 'middle classes' betrays her years in the UK, as well as echoing the middle of the road from earlier. She doesn't even get her weekends off; with her friends all out having fun, she's obliged to spend Saturday nights in the laundromat 'watching the clothes go round': a repeated refrain which the band dutifully take up in the chorus like they're doing backing vocals in the Brill Building.

Indeed, 'fun' is the key. As she jitterbugs around the kind of gritty social realism Ray Davies perfected in 1966 with The Kinks' brilliant 'Dead End Street', she has a ball doing it, her cheerfulness gleefully raising a sour-cream and detergent-encrusted finger to the snooties who laud it over her. The song has a footloose, easy jukebox swing, guaranteed to get her staid diner customers straight out onto the floor. Her overall lot might be straitened and dull, but unlike her frustrated sister from the 'Brass In Pocket' video, she won't be ground down.

'Show Me' 4.09 (Hynde)
The Pretenders again demonstrate their mastery of structuring an album subtly and dynamically, with another distinct shift from the flavour of the

previous track and a perfect example of how to sweeten rock music with intelligent pop. As the band frame a stunning paean to the boss's recently arrived daughter, Robbie's guitar shimmers and shines – the new boy slips into Jimmy's shoes as comfortably as a true brother – while Malcolm and Martin's sterling underpinning could hold up a house.

As expressed in 'Show Me', Chrissie's affection for Natalie has frequently been read as that of a disciple for a religious paragon, even a messiah. This notion has been seized upon by numerous social media pundits. Some have interpreted the song as a bluffer's guide to Christianity (Chrissie equals Christine equals follower of Christ, presumably reincarnating the future Sir Ray Davies as Joseph of Nazareth). But this is over-egging a much less complex premise: though Chrissie welcomes her newborn with an anxious caveat – the human race is riven with wars, disease and brutality – she sees in her daughter's redemptive innocence and grace a conduit to her own deliverance. 'Show me the meaning of the word,' she pleads. It's as if the reassurance she seeks is already compromised by a world which the infant did not choose and that, in its deterioration, has exacted a grievous toll on one of the two people who brought her into it. At two delicious moments, at 2.04 and 3.30, where the tempo rises almost imperceptibly, Malcolm Foster's galloping bass and Robbie's frantically scrubbed lead guitar accompany Chrissie's declamation of the comfort she craves: love.

Chrissie neither deifies Natalie nor uses the little girl as a lazy metaphor. Purely and simply, her unconditional worship is that of a mother for her daughter, who'll restore 'pride and dignity to a world in decline'. The singer's own faith, which we've touched upon, is an entirely personal matter; since she was no more given then to promoting a belief system than she'd tolerate pseudo-spiritual proselytising from others, there's no reason to infer it here.

'Thumbelina' 3.18 (Hynde)
In Hans Christian Andersen's morality fairy tale, Thumbelina is a tiny girl who gains the love of a similarly digit-sized prince after selflessly rescuing a swallow. Here Chrissie projects the wee one onto Natalie, again with a theme of redemption and the triumph of unconditional maternal love. She sings of a mother with her young progeny driving across the US, their destination Tucson (remembering Chrissie's brief sojourn in the Arizona city before even The Pretenders were born). But despite the high spirits – once again, the band are jiving in the juke joint, Martin's shuffling snare and Robbie's reverbed twang powering a jaunty rockabilly – this is more than just another *Easy Rider*-style American road trip. In trading 'the snowstorms and the thunder and rain' for the desert, mother and daughter are escaping a failed relationship, looking to be born again. Chrissie bids her youngster:

Hush little darling, go to sleep
Look out the window and count the sheep

> That dot the hillsides and the fields of wheat
> Across America as we cross America
> What's important here today
> The broken line on the highway.

It's difficult not to assume the partnership she's fleeing is Chrissie's with Ray. The song's final two lines hint at reasons for its failure, an impasse neither party has yet been willing to discuss. 'What's important in this life/Ask the man who's lost his wife,' she sings rhetorically at the close, suggesting the fracture was more down to her partner's slipshod inattention than any carelessness of her own. It doesn't feel as if she's self-berating, even if posterity could still reveal the chemical breakdown to be entirely mutual. For now, as mother takes daughter's hand, striving to 'make it through this world', the sunlit uplands beckon as if over the horizon of a fairy tale.

'My City Was Gone' 5.25 (Hynde)
In 1984, when Rush Limbaugh assumed the lyrical sentiments of 'My City Was Gone' accorded with his own, the late presenter bowdlerised the piece for his radio show's theme tune, demonstrating once again the recurrence of misappropriated rock songs along the less self-aware reaches of rightwing American politics. Perhaps thinking all creative people shared their enlightened opinions, Reagan and Trump both tried it on, respectively, with Bruce Springsteen's 'Born In The USA' and The Rolling Stones' 'Start Me Up'. When Chrissie Hynde discovered Limbaugh's petty larceny, she insisted the broadcaster pay her favourite charity and right-on cause, People for the Ethical Treatment of Animals (PETA), $100,000 in royalties.

The 45th President's habitually sticky fingers obliged his attorneys to deal with cease-and-desist letters from The Stones, Adele, Aerosmith, Johnny Marr, Sinéad O'Connor, Rihanna, Tom Petty, Neil Young, Linkin Park and REM. Limbaugh's lawyers received, if not exactly Chrissie's blessing, at least a tacit approval, due mainly to her late father's regard for the garrulous shock-jock. (Chrissie also later stated that she sanctioned Limbaugh's mishandling because he shared her support for PETA's opposition to an animal testing programme run by the Environmental Protection Agency.) After the Prez granted the terminally ill broadcaster the Presidential Medal of Freedom in 2020, she wrote in a part-conciliatory, part-imploring open letter to the White House:

> The other day, when you gave that award to Rush Limbaugh, my father would have been so delighted. He loved listening to Rush, which is why I allowed my song 'My City Was Gone' to be used on his radio show. My father and I didn't always see eye-to-eye. We argued a lot. But isn't that the American way? The right to disagree without having your head chopped off?

Limbaugh later claimed that he only chose 'My City Was Gone' because he relished the 'irony' of resetting the song to the political right and thus appalling its writer, whom he thoughtfully described as an 'environmentalist, animal-rights wacko'. Disingenuous hindsight and cheap insults aside, the presenter at least had the good taste to praise the song's 'instantly recognisable' intro. It's a great bassline from Tony Butler (remembering the briefly extant lineup that cut the 'Chain Gang' single, of which this was the B-side) over Martin's crashed and reverbed snare and, a few bars in, twangy lead from Billy Bremner. The song lopes along beautifully; were The Pretenders given to such things, they could readily have used 'My City Was Gone' as a vehicle for a half-hour onstage improvisation. The Pretenders might not be Traffic or The Grateful Dead, but its five-odd studio minutes still permits fine, spidery Telecaster soloing from Bremner. A brooding, slightly downbeat feel seems to fit the industrial aftermath evoked by the lyrics. Like the steadily managed decline of a once-proud manufacturing base, the regression is slow and inevitable, the bang at the beginning bleeding out to a desultory whimper and finally ebbing away: the once-fruitful tide that may never return.

Cool basslines and libtard wind-ups aside, it's hardly surprising that Limbaugh thought the song suited his worldview. Chrissie lays to rest, at least for a while, her dreaded/beloved Ohio. Like much of America's modern product, little here is built to last. The once flawed, human, dangerously exciting teenscape of leather, denim, grease, gangsters, hookers, Mosrite guitars, flathead Harleys, trailer-trash, dope, nighthawks and scumbags is now in hock to a bland gentrification, a shiny proto-dystopia with all the planned obsolescence of an '82 Cimarron.

Chrissie told *Blue Railroad* that her sometimes Ohio-centric songwriting was a lifelong obsession:

> I've tried to go back to the Midwest and rebuild those downtowns. I've thought about it for hours and hours. I've thought about what happened to America for years. Then I finally concluded that the way we got that land is where we went wrong. We stole that land, and we built our cities on burial grounds. So those cities had to go. Karmically, we committed an act of genocide. And what you put out came back. So those cities just couldn't live.

Arguably Limbaugh's only 'irony' is that the projected urban decay, which apparently caused poor Rush so many sleepless nights, is the by-product of the free-market, low-tax, small-state politics he so vocally espoused:

> I went back to Ohio
> But my pretty countryside
> Had been paved down the middle
> By a government that had no pride

The farms of Ohio
Had been replaced by shopping malls
And Muzak filled the air
From Seneca to Cuyahoga falls
Said, a, o, oh way to go Ohio.

'Thin Line Between Love And Hate' 3.44 (Rich & Bob Poindexter/J. Members)

A rare Pretenders adaptation that wasn't already the work of The Kinks, 'Thin Line' was originally a 1971 R&B/retro doo-wop hit for the New York vocal group The Persuaders. It's an unusual choice – and another piece that contrasts starkly with its fellows before and after – but Chrissie Hynde was never one to tack towards the obvious, and anyway the words sit comfortably with a theme explored more than once on the album.

Again a relationship is on the skids, the singer weary of her errant man for persistently staying out late and spurning her stoical wifely attentions. Finally, however, her patience runs out and she goes postal. The doomed spouse fetches up nearly dead in the hospital, 'bandaged from foot to head'.

Yet there's a twist. In the Persuaders' original, this little slice of urban gothic is played out from the perspective of the male. Clearly badly injured, he's now the mummified philosopher of the emergency room, sorrowfully contemplating the eponymous fine line and how his infidelities have tipped his wife over its edge. Perhaps it was the way of things in 1971 – more broadly, in certain genres of popular song – but his message seems misogynist, self-pitying and self-serving. He knows he's pushed her too far, but any remorse he might be feeling is expressed in little more than a ruminative shrug. Tacitly he warns others contemplating similar deceitfulness that they, too, could be 'fooled' by their woman and end up like him.

Chrissie redresses the balance in favour of the real victim, altering the original lyrics in order to observe events from a third party's point of view. While she preserves the 'thin line' theorising, she's properly scolding of the wayward husband, her dispassion intensifying to contempt by the song's end. 'You didn't think the girl had the nerve, but here you are,' she sings, although it's uncertain who the barbs are really aimed at, Ray Davies being possibly too obvious. The piano-led arrangement feels authentically 1960s/70s, slightly faster than The Persuaders' version, with heavy gated drum accents from Chambers but neither a McIntosh nor a Bremner in sight. The original had an orchestral score; in the hands of The Pretenders, it's easily imagined but never missed.

'I Hurt You' 4.40 (Hynde)

The album's low point, 'I Hurt You' is grounded in a grumbling bassline seared through by spikes of guitar, plodding its way through a lyrical litany of pain. It's like The Pretenders are so certain of their core audience's benevolence that they've allowed certain parts of their physiognomy to sag, as if the band were a marriage on the rocks without a relationship counsellor in sight. The arrangement features two nicely judged solos from Robbie, but these do little to relieve the lumbering sourness: the lyric arrives halfway through a domestic, straight after the disagreement about what's on telly but just before someone throws the first vase.

Blunt objects or not, the likely victor is fairly clear: 'I've been crying, like a woman, 'cause I'm mad, mad, mad like a man,' Chrissie growls, following through with a vial of vitriol as toxic as ever she cooked up: 'If you'd been in the SS in '43, you'd've been kicked out for cruelty.' The barbs continue, from referencing his 'correction mistress', to a catty implication that his taste in popular TV drama runs no deeper than *Dallas*. Most telling of all, however, are the dope references.

Heroin, once the jazz drug, was now depressingly familiar among rock 'n' rollers. Chrissie's earlier years with the Cleveland demimonde were liberally peppered with as many hardline junkies as (relatively) benign acid-heads and speed freaks. But the song feels unconcerned with blurred one-nighters at the Heavy Bikers' HQ, or later clandestine arrangements beneath boardroom tables. This is a household dispute, maybe even the last in a long and troublesome line.

In terms of the singer's more recent romantic history, Ray Davies' most intoxicating tipple was probably just that, a drink. So it's tempting to conclude, should one allow prurience to trump forensics, that the song's aberrant partner is Pete Farndon. But that prompts more questions: would she decry so venomously a years-past and once cherishable relationship? Especially one with a bandmate whose subsequent death would presumably have inclined her to focus more on the good times than the bad? Whoever this guy is, she's not happy with him. And it shows.

'2000 Miles' 3.38 (Hynde)

On the evidence of numbers alone, successful pop stars who reject the annual teachings of managers keen for Christmas chart action are relatively few. Since only free-jazz tenorists and hair-shirted Stakhanovite bongo players spurn the royalties amassed from persistent appearances on Yuletide compilation CDs – hell, even Bob Dylan figured the world couldn't live without another Christmas album – the least we as consumers have a right to is a palatable outcome. Provided the festive hit avoids the gooey schmaltz of a Michael Bublé or the crazed bawlings of a Noddy Holder, a few of us should be able to stagger from Halloween to the 26th without doing time for aggravated assault.

The Pogues managed it famously. So did John & Yoko, Elton John and Band Aid. The Pretenders' own sits easily among that happy throng, the band for once closing an album not with a bass-centric rabble-rouser, but with a comfortingly snowy sleigh ride through classically seasonal yearnings. Not that Chrissie was thinking of Christmas when she composed '2000 Miles';

relative to the upbeat wittering of, say, 'Driving Home For Christmas', this is Bible-black antimatter. Despite glistening, Byrdsy guitar fading in like a peal of church bells over a wintry horizon, a light swooshing effect reminiscent of a sledge slicing through snow and an even lighter-touch glockenspiel – did any musical instrument ever evoke the holiday season so beautifully? – '2000 Miles' is less a Christmas verse than a melancholic message of loss.

It's simplistic to assume the words evoke a longing for an absent lover; the story is more complex and poignant. For the lost soul is Jimmy Honeyman-Scott, for whom Chrissie wrote the song a year after his death. (Given the flavours mustered in '2000 Miles', from the jingly arrangement to the lyrical signifiers of season and weather, it feels disingenuous to suggest there were no plans for an assault on the December market. Sure enough, the single was released in the UK on 18 November 1983, peaking at number 15. In America, in a decision almost as mysterious as the Christmas story itself, this eminently commercial tune was consigned to the B-side of 'Middle Of The Road', making number 19 on the *Billboard* Hot 100.)

With its admirable feel for time and dislocation, '2000 Miles' was shaped by a little-known song by Otis Redding. This was confirmed by Chrissie in her liner notes for The Pretenders' 2006 collection, *Pirate Radio*:

> The sense of distance in the lyrics was referring to Jimmy Scott. The song itself was influenced by an Otis Redding song called 'Thousand Miles Away'. [The] connection was another thing I thought everyone would pick up on, and, of course, no-one even knows that song.

Wearing Jimmy's clothes to a T, Robbie wrote the luminous guitar intro (for which Chrissie later conceded he should have been credited) while Martin keeps time with an insistent reverbed rimshot. The melody is among The Pretenders' most beautiful, its effect as exhilarating and diffuse as condensed breath on a crisp, cold winter's morning. Anthemic and elegiac, '2000 Miles' tops out perfectly the rockpile of social comment and personal reflection that makes *Learning To Crawl* every inch as essential as its predecessors.

Associated
Bonus Tracks Included With 2007 CD Reissue Of Learning To Crawl
'Fast Or Slow (The Law's The Law')/'Tequila'/'I Hurt You' (demo)/'When I Change My Life' (demo)/'Ramblin' Rob' (demo)/'My City Was Gone' (live)/'Money' (live)

Selected Reviews
'Fast Or Slow (The Law's The Law)' 3.12 (Martin Chambers)
The Pretenders give the drummer some, both as composer and as lead vocalist. If Martin was asked to man the mic, it's safe to say it wasn't because

Chrissie feared for her day job. But since the song's handclap-punctuated Diddley flavouring graced the B-side of two singles, '2000 Miles' and 'Show Me', perhaps the boss was giving her percussionist two bites at the not-inconsiderable royalties accrued by the band's 45s at that time. Whatever, it's enjoyably diverting.

'When I Change My Life' 4.40 (Hynde)
A slower, lengthier demo of the ballad that would later appear on *Get Close*. Produced by Chris Thomas, this crucially lacks the electronic tinkering Bob Clearmountain would eventually use to drag the song kicking and screaming into the mid-1980s. As Ben Edmonds observes in his sleeve notes to the *Learning To Crawl* reissue, 'This is more the way the original band might've arranged it, a close cousin of 'Birds Of Paradise' from *Pretenders II*.'

'Ramblin' Rob' 3.31 (Robbie McIntosh)
A pleasant, work-in-progress instrumental demo knocked off by Ramblin' Rob McIntosh at Denmark Street Studios. The repeated bridge suggests some familiarity with 'Up The Neck' and even, duly adapted, one or more later Pretenders songs.

Get Close (1986)

Personnel
Chrissie Hynde: guitar, vocals
Robbie McIntosh: guitar
T. M. Stevens: bass
Blair Cunningham: drums
Bruce Thomas: bass ('My Baby')
Mel Gaynor: drums ('My Baby')
Pat Seymour: keyboards ('My Baby', 'Tradition Of Love', 'Hymn To Her')
Chucho Merchan: bass ('When I Change My Life', 'Dance!', 'Don't Get Me Wrong', 'Hymn To Her')
Simon Phillips: drums ('When I Change My Life', 'Tradition Of Love', 'Hymn To Her')
Paul 'Wix' Wickens: keyboards ('When I Change My Life', 'Don't Get Me Wrong')
Carlos Alomar: percussion, synth programming ('Light Of The Moon')
Bernie Worrell: keyboards ('Light Of The Moon', 'Dance!', 'I Remember You', 'How Much Did You Get For Your Soul', 'Chill Factor')
Bruce Brody: organ ('Dance!', 'Hymn To Her')
John McKenzie: bass ('Tradition Of Love')
Shankar: violin ('Tradition Of Love')
Steve Jordan: drums, percussion ('Don't Get Me Wrong')
Tommy Mandel: synths ('Hymn To Her')
Martin Chambers: drums ('Room Full Of Mirrors')
Malcolm Foster: bass ('Room Full Of Mirrors')
Rupert Black: keyboards ('Room Full Of Mirrors')
Produced at Air Studios, London; Power Station, New York; Bearsville Studio, New York; Right Track, New York; Polar Studios, Stockholm, by Bob Clearmountain, Jimmy Iovine, Steve Lillywhite ('Room Full Of Mirrors')
Engineers: Bruce Lampkov, Howard Gray
Released: October 1986 (UK); November 1986 (US)
Highest chart position: UK: 6, US: 25

> I don't know of any band that has lasted for 40 years with the same lineup and consistently made interesting, good records. We'd already thrown Pete out and that was after two albums. You've got to change it up. It's just a fact of life.
> **Chrissie Hynde, *Rolling Stone*, 2020**

In his entertaining 2013 single-decade-condensed-to-single-day-at-Live Aid primer *The Eighties*, style pundit Dylan Jones observed how state-of-the-art recording technology now enabled successful pop artists to revisit their original verve and inspiration:

> This is not just the result of rapidly improving studio wizardry – proving to their fan base that they can still sound like they did the day they first rushed

out of the traps – but also the desire to recapture that first flush of fame when their records had the blessing of novelty as well as distinction. The Pretenders are one such example.

Although the author was comparing The Pretenders' first album with *Break Up The Concrete* – if that 2008 record's safety-first rockabilly captured 1979's punkish disorder so faithfully, I must have missed it – perhaps Dylan was still sleeping off Live Aid's after-party 15 months later, on the release of *Learning To Crawl*'s follow-up. For *Get Close* is to *Pretenders* what the similarly urbane *Avalon* is to the splintered and deliciously inventive *Roxy Music*: in each case, two albums self-evidently with the same well-manicured fingers at the tiller – give or take a few adjustments wrought by the years to the respective help – but both a little too fresh from the dry-cleaner and palpably different from their earlier equivalents in tone, structure, intent and realisation.

The Pretenders had, of course, triumphantly cemented their status as rock royalty on the Philadelphia leg of Bob Geldof's 1985 transatlantic charity epic. Live Aid was barely a month past when Chrissie took a sabbatical to re-tread the old Sonny & Cher standby 'I Got You Babe', accompanied by the reggae-lite popsters UB40. Full-on showbiz, the single made number one in the UK (number 28 on *Billboard*) and gave Chrissie the opportunity to trade starry-eyed moves on *Top Of The Pops* with the Birmingham band's singer, Ali Campbell. It could have been Diana Ross and Lionel Ritchie all over again.

Back on Planet Pretenders, the period following the release of *Learning To Crawl* had been uncertain. Despite (or because of?) the band's accomplishments, Chrissie told *NME*'s Paul Du Noyer that she'd like to be more ambitious, 'but I've gotten kind of lazy. I'm doing the same old thing. I haven't thought in terms of a different kind of sound or approach.' By the time the new long-player was begun at London's Air Studios (for one track only before everyone split for facilities in Sweden and the US), she'd reached a decision. With tragedy behind her, the book well and truly closed on Pretenders Mark 1, Chrissie would now embrace the future by whatever means would best fit the band's battered credo. Emboldened by Live Aid, the success of the previous album and its associated singles, not to mention the UB40 interlude's validation of official solo-star status if only she wished or admitted it, Chrissie had enough in the tank to ring dramatic changes. They would resonate for many years.

Get Close marks the moment in The Pretenders' saga when band gets closer to brand, and a conventionally homogeneous quartet melts into something more fluid – Bob Fripp's 'way of doing things', perhaps. The 1980s were buffing everything up to a non-confrontational, digitally compressed gleam; if there was a mismatch, just blame it on the algorithm. The first track to be recorded for *Get Close* was the final sequence's last, a cover of Hynde hero Jimi Hendrix's 'Room Full Of Mirrors'. The song's lineup of Chrissie, Martin, Robbie and Malcolm, bolstered by touring keyboardist Rupert Black, looked like an optimistic nod to continuity following *Learning To Crawl*. Two years on, however, the suddenly urgent quest to adjust the way of doing things, but without frightening the horses, left little unscathed.

In the control room, Chris Thomas was history. He was succeeded at first by Steve Lillywhite, then later by Bob Clearmountain and Jimmy Iovine. If Hynde was indeed busy with a Stalinist purge of apparatchiks whose asset value was suddenly out of step, it was mildly perverse that the Fifth Pretender himself should be sidelined, considering the often dizzying heights Thomas had helped the band to scale. But change was nigh and Lillywhite was flavour of the month. He'd already collected call sheets from The Rolling Stones, XTC, U2, Talking Heads and Peter Gabriel (for whose 1979 solo album he and engineer Hugh Padgham had developed gated reverb, that much-maligned 1980s percussive signifier that would so distance the new Pretenders album from its predecessors). If transformation was nigh, Steve was the man to deliver it. As it was, Lillywhite recorded only the Hendrix cover. Chrissie now inducted the similarly decorated Clearmountain, who could boast such past clients as The Stones, Bruce Springsteen, Paul McCartney, The Who and – interestingly, given the singer's romantic disposition after parting from Ray – Simple Minds.

Chrissie and Simple Minds' singer and co-founder, Jim Kerr, wed in New York City in 1984, shortly after their first encounter in a Sydney hotel lift as their respective groups toured Australia. The age difference was seven years, but this time she was the bona fide star, he the younger, wide-eyed fan. 'Growing up, I had a crush on Chrissie, and I ended up marrying her,' Kerr proudly told *The Sydney Morning Herald* in 2016, conjuring a surreal, looking-glass image of Chrissie's previous relationship. 'As a teenager, I saw a woman who was tough and could front a band. In those days, there weren't many women doing what she was doing.' From the beginning, things looked shaky: days into the compact, Chrissie pregnant with the couple's first and only child, Jim took off with his band on a two-year world tour. Unlike her storm-lashed four years with Davies, Chrissie's first proper marriage barely registered on the Richter Scale of rock relationships, but this may have been because the pair got together so rarely that the landslips were relatively few. They did, however, take time out to produce Chrissie's second daughter; Yasmin Paris Kerr was born on 25 March 1985. 'Getting married to Chrissie seemed like the natural thing to do, but it was hard,' the youngster's father lamented. 'I was always on the road, and when I'd come back, she was on the road. You can't keep a relationship going like that.' The pair divorced in 1990, after Jim left Chrissie for the presumably less busy actor, Patsy Kensit.

Of Chrissie's final estrangement from Ray, both have maintained a civil but Trappist silence. Respective memoirs reveal little; their authors were naturally unwilling to feed the media carnivores any more red meat than necessary. But as Pretender decoupled from Kink (she let Ray go by telephone), a mother's primeval urge to devote time, energy and emotional resources to her daughter stirred in Chrissie a newly grown-up approach to her profession, even if she could still cuss like a drunken stevedore whenever a journalist posed an asinine question. It's perhaps inevitable that, almost overnight, she renounced smoking, drinking and drugging and began the metaphysical leaps of thought that would culminate in her conversion to Hindu Vaishnavism (devotion to which faith Chrissie would celebrate lyrically on the new album's 'Tradition Of Love' and, possibly, numerous other tracks). By accident or design, her music was newly purified, an antiseptic paragon of the age emerging as she cauterised the warts and blemishes.

Biology might also have bred in Chrissie an instinctive resistance to the rock 'n' roll indulgences routinely practised, in defiance of the years, by sexual opposites with whom mature emotional parity is traditionally scant. Imagine an 11-year-old girl shrewdly evaluating the schoolyard talent with her friends, but only after getting her homework in on time. Imagine also her quarry, lurking bashfully with his mates, his homework in the dog. Later on, with life's demands on masculinity often more elective than emergency, the lads can overindulge and hope they leave a beautiful corpse. Great survivors such as Iggy Pop and Keith Richards might limp into the long haul propped up by their ironclad constitutions, but if serial rock 'n' roll party animals don't check out before 30, they risk decaying slowly and horribly. As age compounds the risks, are male or female rock stars the more likely to be overdoing the alcohol and narcotics decades after they should have stopped? To put it another way, had he been around to do so, at what point compared with Chrissie Hynde would Pete Farndon have called time on his abuses? (Paradoxically Chrissie would still be throwing shapes in 2023 at the Glastonbury Festival, at 72 gamine, ludicrously fit, unpardonably beautiful and a glowing testament to abstinence and the Fitbit. But then, even Iggy and Keef managed to get clean eventually.)

Of consequence hardly equal to Chrissie's womanly priorities, but from the band's perspective still a bombshell, was the enforced departure of Martin Chambers. On the drummer's removal, Jimmy Iovine (a respected engineer-producer and future label chief, who now seemed to be acting as father-confessor to a fragile Chrissie) advised the leader that the rhythm section wasn't working. Any implications of glitches with Martin's drumming, which Chrissie critiqued with characteristic bluntness straight after the 'Mirrors' session, were later softened, if only slightly, by her acknowledgement of how hard he'd taken the deaths of their bandmates. As she told Chris Wade of *Hound Dawg* magazine in 2010:

> Martin was playing crap. Martin just fucking lost it, and to think about it, why shouldn't he? He'd just lost his two best friends. I was insane. I was traumatised. But you don't know it at the time. I was trying to keep my shit together. To be honest, Martin was playing crap and I knew musically I was losing my inspiration. But I'd tried too hard and come too far to let it all go, so Martin went instead.

Martin did not accept that his playing had deteriorated. Neither was the shortfall alleged by Hynde triggered by grief. Instead he detected a pretext for empire-building. As he told *MusicRadar* in 2017, Chrissie's ambitions for the Dear Leadership might have lain dormant between 1978 and 1984, but now they were explicit:

> Chrissie wanted to sack me and take charge; that's about as simple as it can get. I understood that, but the way it was done wasn't like that. It was like hacking me off at the knees and insulting me to a point. They didn't want me there because I was taking 50%. I was sent off to Palookaville.

It's possible Martin's natural enthusiasm was waning. But this was the musician deemed important enough, following his Captain Willard-*Apocalypse Now* moment in 1981, for his bandmates to cancel tour dates rather than brief an understudy. His dismissal appeared to be a considerable volte-face by a bandleader on record as an enthusiastic fan. (Following a six-year leave-of-absence in the country, Martin would be asked by Chrissie to rejoin in 1994.) Joining Chambers in podunk limbo was Malcolm Foster, who downed tools in solidarity with the expelled drummer. Explaining away a resignation letter likely to dismay bassists everywhere, Foster told Michael Leonard of *Guitarist* in 1990: 'My whole argument was that Martin Chambers was the rhythm section of The Pretenders and it really didn't matter who was playing bass. So I just said I didn't want to be involved anymore.' Foster – in The Pretenders' universe himself a veteran, having been Chrissie's favourite to replace Pete Farndon in 1982 – was hired by his ex-boss's husband for Simple Minds in 1989. Whether the appointment was Jim Kerr's snub to his imminently ex-missus is unrecorded.

Replacing Malcolm in The Pretenders was T. M. Stevens, of whom Miles Davis had thought highly enough to deploy to one of his electric jazz sessions. Martin's substitute was another ripened funkster, Blair Cunningham, most recently drumming behind Nick Heyward's fey Beckenham popsters Haircut One Hundred, but who could also claim a grittier palmarès in his native USA with Denise La Salle, Frederick Knight and The Detroit Emeralds. The new rhythm section, alongside McIntosh and Hynde, would comprise The Pretenders' latest four-piece, although as the album ripened, the portals of more than one studio would echo to the exultation of numerous other session divines. Carlos Alomar (guitarist with David Bowie, herein tasked with percussion and programming, claiming co-authorship of one track), John McKenzie (gifted former bassist with Man and Annette Peacock *et al.*, nephew to the legendary jazz singer Annie Ross), Simon Phillips (sometime Toto and multi-limbed, much-in-demand drummer) and Bernie Worrell (keys, with Funkadelic, Jack Bruce and counting): all gave of their best so that *Get Close* may live.

How vigorous was that life, despite the talents on display, remains the topic of heated debate among loyal Pretenders fans and a more neutral critocracy.

The overall impression *Get Close* offered the author was that, while clearly a confident, proficient suite of craftsmanlike 1980s songs, the new regime seemed to be chucking out the grease and grime with the sump oil, cleansing the very properties that informed much of The Pretenders' original appeal. Be it related to child-rearing, growing old gracefully (sort of) or both, for the first time the band were erring on the side of caution. The sense of jeopardy, the gambles Chrissie Hynde once risked with rhyme, metre and lyrical acceptability, now lounged comfortably above a safety net of technology and outsourcing. MIDI programming, dependable session players and content that wouldn't frighten the horses if it were hitched to an explosives wagon in an electrical storm – all ensured *Get Close* was absorbed fully into the spirit of the 1980s.

Given the smarts and slickness, it seems almost churlish to criticise *Get Close*. A couple of atypical moon-junes aside, for the most part Chrissie's songs are still on point. Her grasp of a well-turned lyric is not threatened by the album's three non-originals, the most on any Pretenders album so far. On a finely wrought record whose antecedents and reference points have been updated to the forms and feelings of the moment, one can even sometimes forget it's The Pretenders altogether: just cuddle up and get close to *Get Close* for its own zeitgeisty sake. But if the trick is to lie back and think of Japan, lying back and thinking of 'Kid' or 'Precious' or 'Mystery Achievement' or 'The Wait' is a stretch. Awash in synths, the old eccentricities expunged, the incessant bludgeoning by the Panzer beats into a digital air freshener can be overpowering. If you've kept the faith since 1978, it might all end in tears.

Consumers were happy to be coddled, especially in America. Two singles hit number one on *Billboard*'s Mainstream Rock chart: 'Don't Get Me Wrong' b/w 'Dance!' (number ten in the UK) and the US-only 'My Baby' b/w 'Tradition Of Love'. 'Hymn To Her' b/w 'Room Full Of Mirrors', unreleased in the States, made number eight in Britain. *Get Close* charted throughout the world, peaking at number eight in the UK and number 25 on *Billboard*. On the album's reception, Robert Christgau bemoaned Chrissie's newly grown-up approach to her calling: 'It's hard to make exciting music out of a mature relationship, even when fronting a band is the meaning of your life,' sniffed the self-styled Dean of American Rock Critics, before conceding that the 'tunes are up to par' and the lyrics are 'pretty mature.' In 2016, *Classic Rock* was generally positive, recognising the 'radical musical transition by the group firmly controlled by [Chrissie Hynde]'. Then the magazine spoiled it all with the preposterous idea that 'when McIntosh quit in 1987, The Pretenders were effectively finished as a working band.'

As for the leader, Chrissie was pleased as punch with the outcome, as she told Mary Turner of *Off The Record* in January 1987:

> I'm glad the album's out. I think it's a particularly good one. There are some great performances on it. And even if someone doesn't like my voice or my input, or the band's sound in general, no-one can get away from the fact that

some of the drumming, the guitar playing, the overall thing has some brilliant performances. Y'know, I'm delighted to have been part of it.

Chrissie was less impressed by the sleeve photo. She took a similar line, in rather less macabre circumstances, to the doubts she had expressed over Pete Farndon's partiality to the archetypal rock 'n' roll image (see chapter on *Learning To Crawl*). On her own photographic likeness, she advised Turner: 'When I look at that picture, I think that's not me, that's just a picture. I don't relate to it that strongly.' That portrayal, and those on the reverse, strengthen the notion of a woman alone, if a highly successful one. (Thirty-four years would pass before the sleeve of a Pretenders album, 2020's *Hate For Sale*, again depicted all four band members together.) An isolated Chrissie dominates the front cover in a fashionably big-shouldered jacket, hula-hoop earrings and her blue Telecaster. It's a telling image, given the boss's historic resistance to being photographed without her compadres. Richard Haughton's shot is deep-etched against a white background. On the back, Milady's three loyal retainers of the day, McIntosh, Stevens and Cunningham, dutifully line up with their instruments as if queuing at the tradesmen's entrance. The inner sleeve features two mono shots of a relatively collegiate Pretenders – the pics are almost identical, next-door neighbours on David Montgomery's contact sheet – wandering casually along an upmarket London residential street. With his tatty jeans and black biker jacket, Robbie still looks like an old-school – or old-Pretenders – rocker. Otherwise it's designer threads all the way. It was probably an accident of time and place, but the Rolls-Royce parked in the nearby drive seems to speak volumes. (One for trivia-coincidence buffs: David Montgomery also snapped Jimi Hendrix for 1968's *Electric Ladyland*; *Get Close* featured 'Room Full Of Mirrors', the first of three Hendrix covers by The Pretenders.)

'My Baby' 4.07 (Hynde)
According to numerous pundits, *Get Close*'s first track eulogises Jim Kerr. Perhaps they're right: Chrissie sings of her subject getting 'to the heart of the music' and writing 'the beautiful songs'. Yet these are metaphorical devices sitting among couplets that betray less the love of a woman for her spouse, more of a mother for her child.

Two years into their marriage, there's no reason to believe that Chrissie has lost all affection for Jim, even though in a later song on *Get Close* she ruefully takes her husband to task for his persistent absences. But the words 'My Baby' are not intended for a partner. Too maternally tender, they're those of a parent who's overawed by the little human she's so privileged to be raising in her image. And she, perhaps, is too knowing, despite a tendency occasionally to stray from the usual Hyndeian invective into sentimentality.

Ironically the eponymous toddler is not a metaphor. For once in pop music history, here is a song about a baby who's not merely another adult upon whom the writer has romantic designs. By 1986 Natalie was three, so the infant in question is probably Chrissie and Jim's daughter, Yasmin. Her mother's words, among the sweetest Chrissie has written, honour the little girl:

> I seen you dancin'
> A natural beauty
> You make this dive
> Seem sublime
> You really get
> To the heart of the music
> You're the poetry of time.

It's a shame, however, that the music does less justice to the lyrical charm. Once the nutcracking gated sledgehammer has crashed in after barely five seconds, there's no letup; the drums are front and centre, giving no quarter. Robbie counters the onslaught with janglingly pretty guitar figures that could've been outtakes from the final track on *Learning To Crawl*, but it's an uphill struggle. It's dumb to wish it, but what if Yasmin were old enough to have been exalted by the original Pretenders, or the band that made *Learning To Crawl*? The silliest moment, however, comes late in the song: as Chrissie sings, 'To just turn the page, like walking onstage,' an adulatory audience roars as if England has just scored at Wembley. Either it's a clunky sound effect to accompany the words, or a cheap trick to suggest 'My Baby' was recorded live at a stadium concert. Neither is worthy of The Pretenders.

The single's dismal showing in the UK charts – backed by a remix of 'Tradition Of Love', it managed no better than number 84 – suggested one of two things: (a) that in getting too down with inappropriate digital technology, The Pretenders had alienated an original fanbase who expected more grit from Chrissie and her men; or (b) that led by a typically cynical press corps only too ready to tear down what they'd built up, too many British record buyers now saw the band as yesterday's papers. A little of both may be true, although as the briefest dip in the over-chlorinated waters of Duran Duran or Bon Jovi would confirm, the market was embracing the antibacterial 1980s stylings with doctoral gusto. America, perhaps rewarding Chrissie as one of its own, was more forgiving, planting 'My Baby' atop *Billboard*'s mainstream rock chart.

'When I Change My Life' 3.38 (Hynde)

Chrissie Hynde is nothing if not self-aware. Time and again, she's proven herself searingly adept at owning her traits, foibles, sensitivities and shortcomings, then, as a writer, reporting them back in varying degrees – usually sky-high – of literacy and insightfulness. Rarely trite, Chrissie's shepherding of language and implication, in songs about herself or others with whom she feels affinity, has raised such brilliant pieces as 'Up The Neck',

'The Adultress', 'Birds Of Paradise' and 'The English Roses'. These are the kind of Hynde confessionals that frequently tuck real emotion behind wry irony, savage put-down and danceable, rama-lama rock 'n' roll.

Her impulse ever to reflect upon, and reassess, self and circumstance is usually embedded in either poetic metaphor or stubborn opacity. But with 'When I Change My Life', her truthful self-effacement tips over into stating the bleedin' obvious. A lenient appraisal would have Chrissie pleading forgiveness for a past strewn with error, not feeling the need to dress up in verbosity while keeping the music commercially appealing. More unkindly, the song becomes merely product: fabricated banality to attract a big-selling cover version or two – allowing that a songwriter ought to be able to earn her corn in the monetised era of Big Bang and Gordon Gekko.

Taken straight from the writer's mouth, it's all rather self-pitying, an entirely uncharacteristic capitulation. Her beseeching an unknown partner, past or present, that she'll be a good girl from now on – as other areas of *Get Close* demonstrate, she's in no mood to be petitioning Jim Kerr for forgiveness or much else – comes across as a supine declaration of surrender. At best, she's in traditional, boy-meets-girl-tries-not-to-lose-boy mode, writing a note to her teenage diary. She hopes the return on renouncing swathes of her existence to satisfy another will be the unalloyed joy of belonging:

> When I change my life
> There'll be no more disgrace
> The deeds of my past
> Will be erased
> And you'll forgive me
> Then you will come back
> Hold my hand and say "I still love you"
> When I change my life.

The album often runs on a trade-off between words and music – a duff lyric rescued by a great setting, and vice-versa. 'When I Change My Life' does nothing to buck the trend: a lovely tune lifts Chrissie's words, which she has the decency to deliver superbly, her now copyrighted vibrato beautifully understated and controlled. Her accompaniment is suitably impeccable: clouds of FM-friendly synths (from 'Wix' Wickens, a talented English all-rounder, soon to be ennobled as Paul McCartney's musical director) drift through the song like a ground mist, driven from below by ace Bogota bassist Chucho Merchan (whose weighty, almost overqualified CV extends from a Cambridge BA to animal charities in Colombia) and typically judicious stickwork from Simon Phillips (who's said to have perfected the art of double-kick drumming during stints with Judas Priest, Toto and Frank Zappa). Full marks for the team, then, even if it's *nul points* for the sentiment.

'**Light Of The Moon**' 3.57 (Carlos Alomar/Wayne Raglind/Genevieve Gazon)
Former David Bowie sideman Carlos Alomar told of how he brought to the *Get Close* party a promising song left over from a previous gig:

> I asked if we could redo the song and possibly submit it to The Pretenders for consideration. The lead singer sounded just like Chrissie and I felt it would be a great match. So I sent it to Jimmy Iovine ... he loved it. It so happened that The Pretenders had just finished [*Get Close*]. Somehow, Jimmy convinced Chrissie that 'Light Of The Moon' was a hit, and the next thing I knew, I was on my way to California and the band were being asked to return to the studio. I could not have been happier with the outcome.

Alomar was among the funkmeisters assembled by Bowie for, in particular, two signature mid-1970s albums. Not for the first or last time, The Actor demonstrated an eerie knack for crossing genres, in this case from The Stonesy rock of *Aladdin Sane* and *Diamond Dogs* to the snappy, syncopated grooves of *Young Americans* and the magnificent *Station To Station*: albums as influenced by contemporary 1970s black soul and funk as *The Rolling Stones* had been, in 1964, by rhythm & blues. Whether Chrissie Hynde's own adventures in funk, best demonstrated in regions of *Get Close* if not what followed, were as convincing as the Thin White Duke's, however, is debatable. Bowie was a chameleon by instinct; his music and image were constantly subject to shapeshifting change, and often all the better for it. But Chrissie, like The Stones themselves, had laid down early rules of engagement that ought not to be tinkered with by the artist or – perish the thought! – by anyone else. So well-matched was The Pretenders' best music to Chrissie's core values and personality that any tampering would feel like self-harm and, consequently, be self-defeating. (The Stones, authors of the greatest riffs in history, were no better at navigating certain musical topographies already mapped, with much greater agency, by others. Although they'd proved equal to psychedelia, the truth is out there among The Stones' own funk experiments, such as the dismal *Black And Blue* and *Undercover Of The Night*.)

'Light Of The Moon' is a real earworm, with a great arrangement and some of the album's more thoughtful use of the serried tech available to Bob Clearmountain. But while the producer, Chrissie, Carlos and the band deliver on the musical setting, the song itself is less exciting than Alomar's enthusiasm suggested. Genevieve Gazon's lyrics seem to be lightly modelled on Blue Öyster Cult's investigations into the Long Island band's cod-paranormal, renegade-biker mythos, but without the evolving science-fiction narrative that makes BÖC's universe such strange and compelling fun. Gazon sets up a wafer-thin storyline about seven men mysteriously making off with a village community's savings – so far, so 'Last Days Of

May' – before a hasty descent into the kind of oblique imagery perfectly tailored to the MTV demographic. The words may not actually mean very much, but in their intangible, unresolved tracery of secrets, shadows, a sleeping village and moonlit new beginnings, they play well to the song's other-worldly atmosphere, while begging a pseudo-surrealist, 'Vienna'-style promo video.

'Light Of The Moon' is avowedly a musicians' track. It's an opportunity for the self-styled bassaholic T. M. 'Shaka Zulu' Stevens to shine, as he demonstrates the sharp, liquid chops that helped win him gigs with the Mahavishnu Orchestra and James Brown. He scuttles around underneath Blair Cunningham's insistent, Kashmiri backbeat like a tarantula doing the Can-Can, a nimble foil to all the mayhem, melding beautifully with Bernie Worrell's ethereal keys and Robbie McIntosh's funky guitar (Alomar, himself a guitarist of renown, limits his contributions to synths). Musically 'Light Of The Moon' is one of the album's more regal tracks, even if the words suggest a creeping porphyria. But as *Get Close* progresses, Chrissie's own lyrical sovereignty, normally so reliable, is beginning to look ominously purple.

'Dance!' 6.44 (Hynde)
A lengthily chaotic example of the law of diminishing returns, as The Pretenders (Redux) throw at 'Dance!' not only the kitchen sink but the fridge, the microwave and the entire Victorian plumbing system. The result is an overheated soup of Bo Diddley hambone, Hendrix-style wah-wah, Hammond organ, voices and horns (uncredited – perhaps they're simulacra among Worrell's banks of keys?). There's more than a dash of David Bowie circa *Young Americans*. Robbie's fidgety guitar isn't a million miles from Carlos Alomar's on 'Fame', but with the whole band rattling away like they've grown an extra chromosome, 'Dance!' has little of the sparse audial meadow Tony Visconti so brilliantly ploughed for Bowie. Perhaps all you need to know about 'Dance!' is that Chucho Merchan was paired with Cunningham for percussion duties and that someone reasoned the song couldn't possibly succeed without *two* bassists, Stevens and his tirelessly multitasking Colombian colleague.

Lyrically Chrissie snipes at DC politicians, most likely Ronald Reagan, alluding to the then president as part-performing monkey ('Dance! Like a chimpanzee, dance! In the land of the free') and part-whiskey priest, wired to the electorate by empty promises of a promised land. As socio-political comment goes, it's thin and rushed; given the overall atmosphere is rowdier than a Republican National Convention after the bourbon's run out, the song might have prospered had more thought been given to both words and music.

'Tradition Of Love' 5.23 (Hynde)
Despite a reverential nod to Vaishnavism in the final verse, Chrissie's lyrical chops are still AWOL. Where earlier in her career her songs could be relied

upon to interrogate a basket of thematic tropes and archetypes – heavy bikers, lightweight A&Rs, deadbeat lovers, the loneliness of the long-distance Midwest cocktail waitress, etc – here she carves into the song's solid pillars of sound the kind of sappy, soccer-mom-&-apple-pie sentimentalism that The Pretenders circa 1978 surely would have contrived to leave on the last Camden Town bus.

Once more, Chrissie seems to be writing to a brief, swerving from the original, the whip-smart and the out-and-out batty in favour of competing with Diane Warren and other backcombed confectioners of 1980s vanilla. Only this can explain, if not excuse, the laziness of some of the writing. In places it's as if an early beta test of ChatGPT has been asked to generate a lyric that would ape Chrissie Hynde while inviting a cover version by Celine Dion: 'The moon is in the sky and the stars are out tonight/They shimmer in the pools of your eyes in the moonlight', Chrissie quivers, before a final delve into Sanskrit suggests the object of her devotion – on this song and, perhaps, most of the album – might be no-one of this earth but Chrissie's recently embraced creed's 16th-century founder, one Chaitanya Mahaprabhu. This being the case, how would a Hindu adept respond to a line such as 'Ooh you're nice to touch, lovely to look at' as if it were a sign in Selfridges advising its customers to be careful with the bone china? (Intending no disrespect to Chrissie's undoubted sincerity, it should be noted that John Lennon did something similar at the end of '#9 Dream'; the worshipful incantation 'Ah! Bowakawa, pousse pousse', however, was not an elderly lady calling her cat in for its tea, but a classically Lennonish stream of nonsense.)

Meanwhile, Bob Clearmountain does his best to bury the more subtle arguments proposed by Robbie McIntosh's soloing under a mass of layered instrumentation. 'Tradition Of Love' runs on the big, borderline-overproduction that typifies much of the album, although, to be fair, the impressive arrangement is this time imbued more with drama than with directionless bedlam. It's actually a fine noise if you can pretend the (English) words never happened.

'Don't Get Me Wrong' 3.52 (Hynde)

For some of the reasons offered above, 'Don't Get Me Wrong' could be deemed another example of the imaginative palsy numbing Chrissie Hynde's songwriting as The Pretenders marched onwards and upwards to their second decade. If only it wasn't such a damn good pop song.

Numerous areas of *Get Close* tack perilously close to the Warren model, and it's true that a soupçon of lyrical saccharine is swirling around in here. Chrissie's head is again firmly in the clouds, maybe over her man, or her baby, or her divinity. Perhaps it's the latter, seeing as how she gifted the song to John McEnroe. Judged on the sentiments rather than the actual word formations, the origins of 'Don't Get Me Wrong' and 'Tradition Of Love' could have been identical, the verses subsequently prised apart and given discrete musical settings to obey album length and royalty calculations. That's the cynical view, another accusation of indolence, as Chrissie fishes out of a weathered mental file whatever moon-june clichés can be marshalled in the service of songs she scarcely believes in.

However, this time the charge is groundless. 'Don't Get Me Wrong' is saved by its charm, simplicity and unpretentiousness, proving that a Hynde lyric needn't always be poetically corrosive and that, at her best, she easily has the measure of most songwriters with pretensions to mid-1980s chart greatness. Some lines are lyrical gold, even if depth and meaning sometimes play second fiddle to feel and flavour. As she'd remark to *The Guardian* in a 2023 interview: 'Light refracting? Sometimes, you are just looking for a word that rhymes':

> Don't get me wrong/if I'm acting so distracted
> I'm thinking about the fireworks/that go off when you smile
> Don't get me wrong/if I split like light refracted
> I'm only of to wander/across a moonlit mile.

Carefree as a horse-drawn saunter around Central Park on a summer's day, an irresistible tune pops and crackles happily around a lyric that once again celebrates the euphoria of a new love affair, be it religious or secular. She stole the melody whilst on a flight, as she revealed in 2018: 'I think I nicked one of the top-line melodies from the overhead announcement', she told *Ultimate Classic Rock*. 'Dong-dong-dong-dong ... Welcome to British Airways.'

'Don't Get Me Wrong' is by far the album's most commercial track. A sizeable hit across the world, the single made number ten in the UK, number ten on the *Billboard* Hot 100 and number one on *Billboard*'s Album Rock Tracks. For reasons normally contrary to Pretenders appreciation, it's one of the best.

'I Remember You' 2.39 (Hynde)

Perhaps the clue to who Chrissie remembers in this excellent song is where she substitutes 'can't' for 'cannae'. It's difficult here to make a case for a love song to Vaishnavism, but that tiny, first-verse taste of phonetic Caledonia makes it even harder to assume the subject of the song is anyone other than that proud Glaswegian, Jim Kerr.

If so, Chrissie's words give her husband a good rap, even if the title suggests its writer is gazing wistfully back at the anticipation she remembers feeling as she embarked upon a brand-new love affair, rather than describing the elation of an existing one. She examines various key aspects of the relationship – the first meeting, the first time they spoke, the first time they slept together – the tender thoughts shaded by a touching pensiveness that implies the best has passed:

How do we change so easily?
You'll always be a part of me
I thought you'd never go
It shows you what I know.

The fondness of Chrissie's poignant recall suggests that, notwithstanding Jim's shortcomings (if Jim it is, codified more obviously – and accusingly – two tracks hence in 'Chill Factor'), her feelings remained strong when she wrote 'I Remember You'. Assuming the Kerr connection, it's effectively business as usual, the lyrical structure aligning with the romanticism, for good and for bad, of the two previous tracks. It's even tempting to see the three songs as a trilogy, much as the first four tracks on *Pretenders* suggested a themed link to Chrissie's Ohio youth.

Easier on the musical digestion than some of the more declamatory moments of *Get Close*, 'I Remember You' comes wrapped as a short reggae, driven by synths, Blair Cunningham's metronomic rimshots and some lovely, gently surging Hammond from Bernie Worrell.

'How Much Did You Get For Your Soul' 3.48 (Hynde)

In 1983, Michael Jackson inked a sponsorship agreement with PepsiCo, manufacturers of the delicious, life-giving and massively profitable health cordial. In today's reckoning, the deal would be worth north of $15 million. The infamous song-&-dance man was not the first celebrity to take the sponsor's shilling; artists of various stripes have been propped up by corporate largesse since before the Medicis. But so dismayed was Chrissie Hynde when Wacko prostrated himself before The Man in return for financial assistance that was clearly so sorely needed – the poor fellow only managed to sell a miserly 32 million copies of *Thriller* the year of its release – she criticised the pact in song. Later, her outrage was quoted in *The Pretenders Archives*:

> Why would anyone who had any consciousness whatsoever do an advertisement for Pepsi Cola? It's the crassest form of pollution. People are going out and getting all that dough to endorse some garbage product when they don't even need the money anyway. What the fuck are you gonna do with 15 million dollars? Buy a fleet of Rolls-Royces?

By the time of his death in 2009, Michael (who, in 1989, renewed his vows with PepsiCo for a cool ten mil – an eyewatering $29 million today) was rubbing along on just the two Rollers, although his hardship was relieved by numerous other limos, SUVs, vintage cars and a customised fire truck (presumably in case of a repeat of a 1984 misadventure, when his hair was set alight while he shot a Pepsi commercial).

Since Jackson's groundbreaking budgetary initiatives, of course, few high-rolling rock artists have avoided the blandishments of big business. Everyone from Budweiser to Tommy Hilfiger to Castrol has been pleased to sponsor a Stones tour or two, while according to the booking agent Celebrity Talent International, The Pretenders have themselves been pimped out for weddings, funerals and bar-mitzvahs. But as a comparative novelty in 1986, corporate patronage felt like fair game, even if anyone in showbiz judging it risked being held as a hostage to fortune.

In fact 'How Much Did You Get For Your Soul' is less a condemnation than a mild, indeterminate rebuke. Chrissie's words fall a long way short of libel. There's not a Jackson in sight, and even any legal stormtroopers mobilised by Michael and PepsiCo would be hard-pressed to discern tort in lines such as 'Millions of kids are looking at you, you say let them drink soda pop', the song's only oblique reference to the product. Chrissie expresses her tacit disapproval beneath a wickedly upbeat, on-the-one rhythm, as again the band array the same flavours as Bowie circa 1974. This is Carlos Alomar's wheelhouse, but again there's no sign of The Dame's *Young Americans* sidekick. Instead Robbie McIntosh gets another opportunity to prove that his flair for scratchy funk is as keen as his mastery of twangy rock 'n' roll. Chrissie must have been delighted when, in 1988, one of her heroes, Neil Young, targeted similarly sponsored skullduggery in his song 'This Note's For You'. Although Neil withheld the stars' names to protect the guilty, he was less reticent in calling out the culpable companies.

'Chill Factor' 3.27 (Hynde)
Jim Kerr's mitigation for the failure of his marriage to fellow rock 'n' roller Chrissie Hynde (see above) has started to sound thin. The fact that Chrissie wrote 'Chill Factor' at least four years before the pair broke up suggests not all was well within a mere two of the wedding.

Jim's reasoning might have been credible if there were no kids to worry about. After all, as busy rock stars and employers, how could either party lock precious time and energy into the straitjacket of child-rearing? As a devoted mother of two, Chrissie is in no position to choose, lest she follow suit and abrogate all maternal responsibility – which she isn't about to do. That she should be consigned to home and hearth, caring for the bairns while the old man occasionally brings home the bacon (from Australia, or the US, or wherever else Simple Minds' touring schedule takes him), is the chill factor: a settled step too far, even for someone as socially conservative at heart as Chrissie.

As a creative device – or maybe as a measure of tact; she and Jim were still married, and here she was using a potentially million-selling record to air marital grievance – Chrissie adopts a third-person address to make her points about the wronged woman. It's as if she's a dispassionate observer, rather than the victim, of her man's indifference. The song ends with a damning insinuation: that children who are too young to notice their mother coping alone will nonetheless hero-worship their father one day as he reappears, the wayward prodigal back from far away, his guilt ameliorated with paternal payola. It's a poignant and, in many ways, heartbreaking song, but it's ill-served by one of the most inflated arrangements on the album.

Once again, the gated snare carpet-bombs everything into the next postcode (this time Cunningham's behind the kit, although the buck has to stop with Clearmountain, if not the boss herself). So violent is the percussive blitzkrieg that the words risk losing the poignancy a more sympathetic setting would permit. Positioning herself as a spectator rather than a casualty should allow Chrissie the room to be objective, eschewing her usual anger for philosophical acknowledgement of a bad situation. Since she's part of the same world, she's reflective, understanding her husband's position without exactly being overjoyed about it. Unfortunately, the crucial nuance of one of the album's best lyrics is sacrificed on an altar of ineffectual bombast. In 1995, with Martin Chambers safely back in the fold, Chrissie gave her song the respect it deserved with an 'unplugged' reading of 'Chill Factor', releasing it on a fine live album, *The Isle Of View*.

'Hymn To Her' 4.47 (Meg Keene)

For someone historically so guarded about women's lib – a position that would be subject to adjustment – Chrissie is happy to deliver a song that valiantly taps into pagan concepts of the Eternal Feminine and the Three-fold Goddess: themes beloved of feminists of a Wiccan or otherwise spiritual disposition. Although ambiguous lyrics are flattered by a hauntingly evocative musical setting, 'Hymn To Her' is, by some distance, the best track on *Get Close*, happily avoiding the album's frequent overproduction while doing a stand-up job of sounding cleverer than it really is.

'Hymn To Her' was composed by Chrissie's high-school friend, Meg Keene, a jazz pianist in her youth and, according to *Reckless*, 'the most individual' of Hynde's Ohio posse. Terrible punning title and woolly sentiments aside, 'Hymn To Her' is certainly a promising effort, although Chrissie's captivating vocal, not to mention a glorious arrangement, raises the song to a level that might have surprised its young composer.

Meg's words are vague enough to have invited explanatory overload. As some have earnestly argued, the song proves Chrissie is, or was, a pagan (she's not, although there might have been the occasional youthful dabble, and the writer herself may have had leanings). For others, it relates to down-to-earth ideas of femininity more prosaic than allowed for by pre-*Buffy*, teen-witch esoterica. Others yet detect the menstrual cycle and a fragrant hint of – possibly unrequited – Sapphism. Had the young writer emotionally leaned too heavily on a trusted confidante, be she Chrissie Hynde or someone else? Given Chrissie's brimming charisma, it's easy to imagine the rock-star-in-waiting as a powerful role model and sounding board for impressionable contemporaries at Firestone High. Meg's lyrics, though often confusing, reveal a certain neediness, as if imploring the object of the writer's affections to give more than she's willing:

Let me inside you
Into your room
I've heard it's lined
With the things you don't show
Lay me beside you
Down on the floor
I've been your lover
From the womb to the tomb
I dress as your daughter
When the moon becomes round
You be my mother
When everything's gone.

'Hymn To Her' tries hard to be all this and more. Meg's conceits suggest there was enough space on the Keene bookshelves for Goethe and Graves (Chrissie describes Meg's family as 'intellectual') along with those authors' and others' theories of the Triple Goddess as the embodiment of whole womanhood. Yet the song could be read as another take on the mother-daughter complex that's so exercised Chrissie's thoughts since Natalie's arrival. While Keene's oblique high-school poetry folds Maiden, Mother and Crone into a broader contemplation of womanly tropes and archetypes both feminine and feminist in outlook, however, this could be overthinking it. The song probably isn't as profound as its ambivalent lyrics suggest, despite a sublimely atmospheric setting probably best experienced in the middle of a stone circle under a full moon.

The arrangement of 'Hymn To Her' is memorably gorgeous. It's also relatively spare, allowing the kind of spatial dynamics in short supply elsewhere on this endlessly busy album. Only McIntosh is retained from the core quartet, decorating the shimmering washes of synth, keyboards and cymbals with filigrees of reverbed guitar, while Phillips keeps time with steady rimshots and small tom-tom fills. The backing intensifies at 2.07, briefly scaling the album's wall of sound, then allowing fallback for the later verses. The band swoop back in for a stirring finale before fading out with a short, expressionist, semi-improvised coda. Unreleased as a single in America, 'Hymn To Her' made number eight on the UK top ten, backed by the final song on the album.

'Room Full Of Mirrors' 4.36 (Jimi Hendrix)
Get Close concludes with a lively version of one of Jimi Hendrix's less celebrated compositions. Nevertheless it's an excellent one, played by a Pretenders that had felt relatively settled until Martin Chambers was mysteriously repurposed and Malcolm Foster walked out in support.

Twenty years earlier, the psychedelically-slanted 'Room Full Of Mirrors' had been a testing onstage negotiation even for a group as proficient as Hendrix's Experience. As the legendary guitarist-songwriter's biographer Harry Shapiro put it, 'Jimi had to be three guitarists at once, two lead and one rhythm.' This was a tough call, even for a genius. Still, the Experience and Hendrix's later groups were essaying 'Room Full Of Mirrors' in concert from 1969 until his death in 1970. The song, which Hendrix intended for a later-aborted fourth studio album, remained unavailable on authorised record until it was released the following year with the *Rainbow Bridge* collection. For its first live outing, an eight-minute jam taped at the Royal Albert Hall in 1969 and included on a 1971 soundtrack album, *Experience*, the trio were joined onstage by two members of show openers Mason, Capaldi, Wood & Frog: flautist Chris Wood and guitarist Dave Mason. Input from the latter – himself a fine player – presumably obliged Jimi to grow just the two extra arms.

In the loving arms of The Pretenders, following a brief intro similar in flavour to Japan's 'Quiet Life', the flurry of Chambers' hi-hat and Foster's sequenced bass create a totteringly cliff-edged tension, before Martin crashes through from behind the traps. Despite the inevitable production gloss, The Pretenders' original drummer displays all the muscular, pumped-up gusto the group will have to learn to live without for the rest of the album and, indeed, for the next eight years. Meanwhile Robbie McIntosh hits the effects pedals and slides up, down and around the neck of his Telecaster like a sidewinder on acid.

According to many, entirely predictably, a lysergic high was guiding Hendrix's brain cells when he wrote 'Room Full Of Mirrors'. (Some aver it was his maiden trip, although this is unlikely; Jimi first took LSD in 1966 but penned the song two years later, albeit after several months of laborious work.) The lyrics betray their writer's anxieties over his fame and the adulation and expectations of his fans – worries that were consuming Jimi almost before the Experience's freshman single 'Hey Joe' had completed its chartbusting run early in 1967. It takes no great suspension of disbelief to reason that, at this stage of The Pretenders' journey, the leader of one of the world's biggest rock bands might have sensed similar unease. However she was feeling, Chrissie does her idol proud, flailing around the song's nightmare of self-absorption, lost and trapped down its psychedelic rabbit-hole of ego. As she does so often, she half-sings, half-speaks the words, channelling Hendrix's own style of delivery as she searches for truth, meaning and relevance. Like her hero, she needs to escape a solipsistic life assaulted by myriad congested incarnations of her own personality. Like Pete Townshend's *Tommy*, she finds catharsis in sundering the metaphorical glass, looks beyond herself and busts free into the real world:

> I used to live in a room full of mirrors
> All I could see was me
> Well I took my spirit
> And I crashed my mirrors
> Now the whole world is here for me to see.

Struggling to escape her own multi-reflected incarceration, Chrissie breaks on through the bullshit and picks her way past the hallucinatory shards, uncertain where the resultant cleansing will take her. In pursuit of an answer, it probably doesn't do to make too much of Chrissie's mindset when she recorded the song relative to Jimi's back in 1968. Most likely The Pretenders' interpretation was homage, a favourite Hendrix tune serving as the vehicle for a respectful tribute. Besides, detecting and neutralising acid-fuelled paranoia over spooky mirror images of self would probably need another skipful of psychotropics.

Thankfully such measures were redundant. For all her apparent glacial indifference, thousand-yard stares and a viperish, in-yer-face assertiveness that sometimes overcompensated for chronic shyness, Chrissie was nothing if not a tough-minded pragmatist. By now she understood how to use the bedlam of the rock business to her advantage. She knew the value of a commercial tune that could pay the mortgage, with change; and she had finessed the art of keeping her head far enough above all the craziness to allow her to bring up her children responsibly and lovingly.

By contrast, Hendrix was an incandescent rock 'n' roll ruin waiting to happen. Just 27 when he died, physically slighter than his astonishing, elemental onstage power suggested, Jimi constantly struggled with celebrity and its trappings. From the outset, the gentle fragility that stood in direct contrast to his wildman image inscribed a target on his back for unscrupulous managers, demanding fans, cynical dealers and turbocharged drugs. Small wonder his addictive personality burned so brightly, so quickly, before the end. Like the similarly untimely deaths of Lennon, Jones, Joplin and Morrison – and, lest we forget, Honeyman-Scott and Farndon – Hendrix's tragedy was practically pre-ordained.

Get Close's closing statement is a respectful salute to a signal Hynde influencer, performed by a group whose rhythmic heart was about to be transplanted in pursuit of a shiny new 1980s relevance. Perhaps it's a coincidence that *Get Close*, that pivotal moment of change, climaxes with the one track to retain even a tenuous link with the ghost of Pretenders past. Far from lodging the song at the beginning of the album, as if to get the obsolete and dusty out of the way well in advance of unveiling the new and sexy, 'Room Full Of Mirrors' is sat at the end, The Pretenders' own liminal space, the mid-term between what's been lost (or wilfully discarded) and the brave new world to come.

With their fourth album, The Pretenders had shifted gear in a way that felt unimaginable just a few years before. Chrissie saw *Get Close* as something of a watershed, as she told *Off The Record*:

> I can't say I've ever really been as content after making an album. I'm not sure if I'm hitting my peak in the band or if we're just coming to a turning point. Maybe we're about halfway through the band's career. It's kinda how I'm feeling at the moment, rather than it coming to the end or not really

going anywhere ... I'm starting to feel as if I'm at some sort of a turning point. I feel we're just coming into our stride.

There's no doubt *Get Close* remains a classy pop album. It's played by a cadre of the world's best session hires, exceptionally well-crafted even if the respective quality of words and music are sometimes mutually exclusive. Much as *Learning To Crawl* did such sterling work, under difficult circumstances, to build on *Pretenders* and *Pretenders II*, the next volume will try hard to stay true to the direction established, rightly or wrongly, by *Get Close*. Whether or not *Packed!* succeeds is moot – Chrissie herself will later recall an imminent, if thankfully temporary decline – but one thing is certain: compared with the unruly adolescent of 1978, The Pretenders are now a grown-up and very different animal.

Associated
Bonus Tracks Included With The 2007 CD Reissue Of Get Close
'Hold A Candle To This' (alt)/'World Within Worlds'/'Tradition Of Love' (remix)/'Dance!' (take 1)/'Don't Get Me Wrong' (live)/'Thumbelina' (live)

Selected Review
'World Within Worlds' 3.49 (Hynde)
'World Within Worlds' is a properly exciting rocker that, for some reason, failed to pass the smell test for the final release of *Get Close*. It features blockbuster drumming (likely Blair Cunningham doing Martin Chambers impressions), motorcycle noises and an unusual time signature, as well as oblique lyrics that tell of how a 'flashback of memories [brought] a deep silence' of 'old, glowing stars' and of how 'death opens doors'. With the words possibly referencing the losses of Jimmy and Pete, the arrangement noticeably lacking in the pervasive binary code of *Get Close*, there's a definite whiff of The Pretenders of old. Perhaps that's the reason.

The Pretenders ... *On Track*

Packed! (1990)

Personnel
Chrissie Hynde: guitar, vocals
Blair Cunningham: drums
Billy Bremner: guitar
John McKenzie: bass
Tchad Blake: guitar ('May This Be Love', 'No Guarantee')
Mitchell Froom: keyboards (all except 'Never Do That', 'Millionaires', 'Sense Of Purpose', 'Downtown (Akron)', 'Hold A Candle To This')
Dominic Miller: guitar ('Sense Of Purpose', 'Hold A Candle To This'), bass, backing vocals ('Sense Of Purpose')
David Rhodes: guitar ('Millionaires', 'Criminal')
Tim Finn: backing vocals ('When Will I See You')
Mark Hart: backing vocals ('When Will I See You')
Will MacGregor: bass, backing vocals ('Never Do That')
Teo Miller: backing vocals ('Millionaires')
Tony 'Gad' Robinson: bass, backing vocals ('How Do I Miss You')
Duane Delano Verh: bass ('May This Be Love')
Adey Wilson: backing vocals ('Millionaires')
Produced at Air Studios, London; Mayfair Studios, London; Abbey Road Studios, London; Sunset Sound, Los Angeles, by Mitchell Froom
Engineers: Tchad Blake, Geoff Foster, Rob Jaczko, Teo Miller
Released: May 1990
Highest chart position: UK: 19, US: 48

I have been asked 10,000 times, 'Are The Pretenders just you? Or is it a band?' All I can say is that I'm not a solo artist. My position in any band that I've been in is to set the guitar player up to make a goal. It's all about the guitar.
Chrissie Hynde, *Rolling Stone***, July 2020**

Since Pete and Jimmy died and because I've had to replace people, it's now kind of like a Pretenders tribute band named The Pretenders.
Chrissie Hynde, *Record Collector***, September 2023**

On the surface, *Packed!* is what happens when you get the consultants in to make a rock 'n' roll record. The Pretenders' fifth album, the last shout of a tumultuous decade, once again bursts at the seams with heavy friends and hired hands. The very concept of a regular quartet is history, the scattergun approach to group homogeneity wearyingly familiar. In 1986, Pretenders ultras might have thought the MIDI-funk experiments against the grain, for some even alien. But no-one listening to *Get Close* could accuse the band of having rested on its 'Adultress'-shaped laurels. Now The Pretenders haven't so much run out of road, they just can't seem to be arsed to progress any farther along it.

This was the initial reaction to *Packed!* by many Pretenders fans, including the author. But because the album neither slaps you around the head (like *Pretenders*) nor immerses you in the fallout from a digital bathbomb (like *Get Close*), it's too easy to assume that *Packed!*, in its entirely unassuming way, is a massively inferior product to anything else by the band. In fact, *Packed!* is a grower.

Its music isn't so demanding that acceptance depends upon absorption over time of serpentine structures and awkward signatures. Quite the reverse. After four or five plays you're helplessly humming away, for *Packed!* is unquestionably a pop album. But it's one whose hooks don't always obey the convention that a popular song must prompt instant recall. There's no 'Brass In Pocket' or 'Kid', just a bunch of beautifully produced tunes that arrive out of nowhere and declare squatters' rights in your sensory receptors, whether you like it or not.

Four years before the release of *Packed!*, The Pretenders were on the road in support of its predecessor. Ace keyboardist Bernie Worrell joined Hynde, McIntosh, Stevens and Cunningham. If the touring lineup was all-conquering on paper, however – and Chrissie considered its studio work exemplary – within a few shows the boss was unhappy, belatedly seeing in this treasurehouse of funk the polar opposite of what The Pretenders were about. As she told Chris Wade, 'It wasn't an English pop band any more.' Though superb at their craft, in mid-tour Worrell and Stevens were ousted (harshly, Chrissie later admitted) while Rupert Black and Malcolm Foster were hastily rehired. Cunningham escaped the defenestration, as did McIntosh, although another disappointment awaited at tour's end, when Linda McCartney insisted her husband should hire Robbie with all dispatch.

A further casualty of The Pretenders' late-1980s night of the long knives was manager Dave Hill, with whom communication had irrevocably broken down. Dave was replaced by Paul McGuinness, whose Principle Management had been ordained as U2's pastoral emissaries on Earth. Booking The Pretenders to open 16 US shows for the Hibernian demiurges on their 1987 *Joshua Tree* tour, McGuinness brokered a meeting between the temporarily guitarist-free Chrissie and the prodigiously-talented Johnny Marr, recently unshipped from Manchester miserabilists The Smiths. As Marr explained to u2songs.com in 2018:

> [McGuinness] told me The Pretenders had some gigs lined up supporting U2 in America, and Robbie McIntosh had left; would I do these gigs? That was an interesting invitation because I'd liked The Pretenders' early records, and without a doubt, James Honeyman-Scott was a big influence. I met with Chrissie and we got on really well. The gigs were fantastic. To learn 30 Pretenders songs in a few weeks was a real challenge. On a personal level, Chrissie helped me immensely with the Smiths split and dealing with the press.

Chrissie later said her hookup with Johnny was like finding Jimmy all over again. The euphoria was mutual, but short-lived. A near burned-out Chrissie had relapsed to smoking too much reefer, which bothered her new guitarist-elect, himself often tardy with studio schedules. As soon as the pair tried to get something down on tape, everything went south. Although it would later be rekindled, an all-too-brief relationship that promised so much was abruptly terminated. The pair were at least able to collaborate on tour and on a 1988 single attributed to The Pretenders: Burt Bacharach and Hal David's 'Windows Of The World', included in the soundtrack to the wartime drama *1969*.

Meanwhile Chrissie was spending more time with her activism. At 17 she'd quit eating meat, but 22 years later, to the consternation of *Daily Mirror* readers, her vegetarianism turned militant. At a June 1989 news conference promoting Greenpeace, she puckishly claimed to have firebombed a branch of McDonald's, as you do. Although she was far from serious, not everybody got the joke; unfortunately someone did the actual deed the following day. There were no casualties, but a *Mirror* hack salaciously reported Chrissie's gallows humour as a call to arms. When P. C. Nab dropped by and asked her to account for her impish rabble-rousing, she was advised to stop being beastly to the fast-food giant, an undertaking enforced by injunction and which, no doubt, led to even more of a shortfall in Big Macs on the Hynde dinner table. (Age didn't mellow her disgust, as she later told *Billboard*: 'I don't want to leave this mortal coil until every McDonald's is burned down to the ground.')

Happily there's more nutrition in evidence on *Packed!*, although digesting it takes time. The edginess and vivacity of the early trio of long-players, even the buffed-up professional gleam of *Get Close*, at first feels lost on a search for the line of least resistance. Chrissie, Billy Bremner, Blair Cunningham and John McKenzie go through the motions as a stable lineup, but nods to continuity are few. Drummer Cunningham is the only survivor from *Get Close* to play on all 11 tracks of *Packed!*; guitarist Bremner, last heard on the 'Back On The Chain Gang' single, performs on nine; bassist McKenzie contributes to seven. Otherwise *Packed!* reports for duty with another strong contingent of rock 'n' roll soldiers of fortune.

Like its predecessor, objectively it's hard to identify much wrong with a record that's so well played and sung. Production values align with a migration being felt elsewhere in the recording industry, steering clear of the 1980s artifice that doesn't completely manage to occlude *Get Close*. The guitars – mainly Bremner, with a little help from Chrissie and from Tchad Blake (a seasoned session player frequently partnered with Mitchell Froom) – once more recall a George Harrison or a Roger McGuinn, their lines shimmering in sensual curlicues around arrangements that wouldn't disgrace *Rubber Soul* or *Younger Than Yesterday*.

If there is a problem with *Packed!*, it resides within the lyrics. Chrissie's writing is sometimes parked in the doldrums, her positivity stretched to breaking point on a rack of uncharacteristic self-pity. After five albums, this suggests a need for proper refreshment beyond the usual post-album support tour and yearly Vaishnavist pilgrimage to India. (Following *Packed!* The Pretenders didn't release another album for four years.) More optimistically, though, the arrangements and production of *Packed!* often sparkle with sprightliness. The still-quality songwriting of the previous record escaped being completely smothered by Bob Clearmountain's polished 1980s production. Now some of Chrissie's most downbeat songs to date are lifted with the help of Mitchell Froom and some pretty decent tunes.

California-born producer Froom was another music-industry pro with an impeccable pedigree. A noted session keyboard player and composer of film scores, he played with and/or produced his wife, Suzanne Vega, as well as Elvis Costello, Crowded House, Los Lobos and Richard Thompson. He arrived at Chez Pretenders with a no-nonsense approach to record production: 'Cut the crap; get rid of extraneous elements right away,' Froom told *Rolling Stone*'s Bud Scoppa of his working regimen. This felt as if Froom was sniping at Clearmountain, whose work on *Get Close* was nothing if not relentlessly busy. Yet Mitchell's reductivism proved effective, even if the results weren't balls-to-the-wall exciting in the classic Pretenders sense. 'To make a song interesting,' Froom assured Scoppa, 'I like to think that there's the 'wild element' – what Brian Jones did for the early Stones – where you go for something unusual, but it still works.' *Packed!* is many things, lots of them good, but 'wild', 'unusual' and 'Brian Jones' – elements once abundant even in the more rarified atmospheres of early Planet Pretenders – it is not.

The sad fact is that, despite being very much better than is suggested by a few cursory airings, *Packed!* has become The Pretenders' guilty little secret. Shininess, songcraft, the popular sense that the band were back with a vengeance after the early-1980s Tribulation, a new broom ruthlessly doing its bit for the rebirth: all accorded *Get Close* some critical slack. But critics and many fans have found it hard to extend the same generosity to its put-upon successor. *Packed!* seems to have been plonked rather forlornly amid the merry dance of Pretenders albums, the plain girl at the back of the village hall who can't get a partner. Today the album is rarely paid the compliment of reappraisal, except by the boss herself, who later dismissed its content as 'stupid little pop songs'. But for now, Chrissie's priorities lay beyond the relative trivialities of music-making. She wanted to mother two young children she loved, not assemble three or four musicians and hit the road in support of an album she didn't.

Meanwhile even a 'deluxe' double-CD reissue from 2015 noticeably lacks the usual authoritative essay on the album's origins. And in case of any misunderstanding, the same lavish edition remains a victim of that mercilessly algorithmic mark of consumer indifference, relegation to Amazon's bargain bin. Chart listings were discouraging (except in Sweden, where fans remained sufficiently loyal to send it to number seven). In the UK, it peaked at number

19 and in the US at number 48. The album's dolorous performance was due in part to The Pretenders deciding not to tour, but any notion of a stable, working band was, for now, atomised under the assault of freelance labour. *Get Close* had at least acknowledged the quartet which then officially comprised, more or less, The Pretenders, even if its members were scattered across numerous tracks and Madame claimed the lioness's share of imaging space. For *Packed!* there's no such pretence, other than attributing the record to an entity identified as The Pretenders, despite evidence that, temporarily, no creature of that name existed.

Indeed, suspicions have long abounded that *Packed!* was accredited to The Pretenders merely to satisfy recording industry contract lawyers, and that really this was Chrissie Hynde's first solo album. The football team of session players and, crucially, no real sense of group identity are, of course, coincidental.

The credits and sleeve imagery in *Packed!*'s packaging are more Hynde-centric than ever. For Martin Chambers – his voice not, perhaps, the most impartial, given the then-resting drummer's revolving-door relationship with the band – the leader was spoilt, as he opined to Julian Cope's *Head Heritage* site in 2009:

> One thing she doesn't realise is that it's all been her since about 1986. It's all been her and nothing else. And I think the whole Pretenders thing has suffered because of that. The point is it's The Pretenders. It's not like Neil Young. It's not like Chrissie Hynde and The Pretenders. It's The Pretenders. And yet you have all these albums through the end of the '80s and '90s, and what's on the front? A picture of her. There were still some great songs, don't get me wrong, [some] classics, but not many. She's not the most prolific.

On the front cover of *Packed!*, the lady's hazel eyes glare out from beneath her patented bangs in extreme closeup, the 'Pretenders' masthead reverting to its familiar Art Deco typestyle. On the reverse is a thin visual pun of a pair of packed touring cases, along with instruments and backline, coffee cups and ashtrays sitting unmanned in an untidy rehearsal space. It's as if everyone's suddenly been called away – or packed off? – in mid-practise for a photoshoot whose evidence will never be printed. The inner dust jacket, by famed rock snapper Jill Furmanovsky (a friend of Chrissie's since the salad days of punk), depicts only a t-shirted leader, moodily intent on her heavily airbrushed Telecaster as it apparently bursts into flame. Thankfully the music has enough propellant in the tank to do the same, even if it does take a while to catch.

'Never Do That' 3.20 (Hynde)

In 1972, the Irish singer-songwriter Gilbert O'Sullivan released a single entitled 'Alone Again (Naturally)'. With its dismembered, multi-tracked vocal and major-key jauntiness, the record was built to be successful – which it was, in spades – alongside other chartbusters that year by the likes of the New Seekers and Lieutenant Pigeon. But while those worthies limited their expressions of emotional torment to Coca-Cola and mouldy bread mix, O'Sullivan's words spoke of tragedy, personal loss, religious betrayal, the deaths of his parents and suicide. Yet still yer man bounced merrily up and down behind his piano, wrapping the song into a melody of missives of similar portent, such as 'Clair' and 'Ooh-Wakka-Doo-Wakka-Day'.

The reason I relate this anecdote is to illustrate how a song's musical setting sometimes bears no obvious affinity with its lyrical content. In the case of 'Alone Again (Naturally)', O'Sullivan's disconnect was borderline crass, as could be inferred by watching the teenies on *Top Of The Pops*, all happily bopping away even as Gilbert advised them of how he once contemplated throwing himself off a roof.

While far short of a suicide note, the words of the first track on *Packed!*, delivered by a suitably detached Chrissie Hynde, betray a desultory mood that sails worryingly close to self-loathing. The contrast to the warmth, sparkle and ironic punch of Chrissie firing on all cylinders is stark. The feeling engendered by 'Never Do That' is blanketed in cold grey, pitching the track into a state of indeterminacy, debasing the beginning of the record and threatening to greyscale the next 42 minutes.

She pleads with somebody – a lover? A husband? – pledging to be a good girl if only she's allowed to tarry. The following verse is especially telling, as she dolefully accepts the impasse in which she finds herself, powerless to do anything about it:

> Take my mouth as far as you can see
> It stretches farther than I care to think
> Put me out of my misery
> If I could keep it shut
> I wouldn't be in this rut
> With less chance than a laboratory rat
> Oh no, I'd never do that.

'I won't make a sound, I'll just hang around, I'll sit where the last one sat,' she sang earlier, a mousey wallflower wilting under the studied indifference of an emotional blackguard. Self-pity's not normally Chrissie Hynde's way, but the cheerlessness exposed by the sentiments of 'Never Do That' is hard to get past.

So the words are hardly promising. Yet you'd not know it from the music. Though nothing new, the arrangement mines a seam that, in the wake of the digital enhancements of much of the 1980s, feels natural, vibrant and restorative. The song bears a strong comparison with the music of REM, with whom The Pretenders had co-owned the 1980s without either moving their tanks onto the other's lawn. By 1990, however, a flair for commercial, melodic, Byrdsy college rock had poised the quartet from Athens, Georgia for world domination. For the time being, Michael Stipe's men were the ones to beat.

On the evidence of 'Never Do That', Team Pretenders (like so many others, from Fastball to the Pixies to one Johnny Marr) are picking up on similar minor-key glory. The track has a good, if derivative tune, with a lovely 12-string shine and strummed acoustic rhythm guitar. Meanwhile Billy Bremner's lead is touched up with shivering reverb (a sound that REM would leverage four years later on *Monster*). 'Never Do That' might sound like a similar but slightly inferior reworking of the brilliant 'Back On The Chain Gang', but despite the dour messaging, its musical freshness bodes well for the rest of the album.

The single was accompanied by a typically stylish but meaningless MTV promo video. A rainwear-clad Chrissie scurries through monochrome streets in London and Paris, occasionally interrupted by performance footage. In accordance with the prevailing convention for a band now skeletally trimmed, The Pretenders appear to comprise mainly Chrissie lip-syncing in closeup at the mic, with Blair Cunningham sometimes seen drumming in the back and, nudging into the spotlight from a shadowy stage left, a Stingray bass headstock, presumably with Will McGregor at the other end.

'Never Do That' was the first of three singles culled from *Packed!*, its chart performances emblematic of a slight drift in The Pretenders' standing as a global hits act. America kept relative faith by lodging it at number four on *Billboard* Alternative, while those testy Brits let the side down by sending it no further than number 81. Perhaps we listened too closely to the words, although that never seemed a problem for Gilbert O'Sullivan.

'Let's Make A Pact' 3.18 (Hynde)

Despite an arrangement that's among the sweetest on the album, shot through with skirling Hammond organ and a lustrously insistent folk-rock 12-string, 'Let's Make A Pact' has to do the same heavy lifting as the previous track once the lyrical meanings and inferences are excavated.

The pact in question is marriage, a crucial agent of change that Chrissie can only find beneficial and whose vows she hopes will never be rescinded. She imagines herself wondering at the world, freed to 'dance'; after 'twenty years of doubt, and then a week with you, I'm ready baby'. So far, so good, but this is a long way from a standard romantic proposal, as those self-doubts flow back in like a tidal runoff:

> Empty me
> Like a dustman rids a rubbish bin
> Fill me up with glimpses of you
> And let the music begin
> Oh oh oh
> Take me to the altar.

One can only wonder at Chrissie's feelings in the aftermath of two famous rock 'n' roll relationships and whatever others she was mercifully able to screen off from the public's gaze. When she asks, with rather overheated rhetoric, that she be covered in dirt and left to the wind and the rain if she 'should ever hurt the one who made me human again', it's hard not to be reminded of her compliant younger self. She chronicled her incaution in tales of wreckless indiscretion which, though the threats she faced were hardly of her making, she offered as evidence that she somehow had it all coming and that 'boys will be boys' (especially the *really* bad ones with the Nazi daggers and the prehistoric takes on women's rights). In its own way, 'Let's Make A Pact' lays bare the writer's soul, paradoxically on an album whose content is The Pretenders' safest and least confrontational to date. Is this confirmation of those earlier songs' implications? That the loud, dangerous harpie of the classic group was, beneath it all, really a submissive female nebbish, the unassuming waitress in the Akron diner, content to allow men to be men and women to be glad of it? With a personality as powerful as Chrissie Hynde the idea is unlikely, but given her equally obvious complexities, not impossible. Perhaps the motorcycle gang with guitars really was a façade for something a lot more nuanced than all the strut 'n' bluster suggested.

The second song on *Packed!* provides the album's punning title, although the reasoning appears to be of little more significance than a convenient play on the words that appear as Chrissie writes.

'Millionaires' 3:04 (Hynde)

John Lennon's 'Imagine' syndrome all over again, then: a prosperous rock 'n' roller ambushes those more comfortable with balance sheets than music sheets and rushes to occupy the moral high ground. It's true that the cups of property developers rarely overflow with the milk of human kindness, and successful rock musicians can be every inch as venal and grasping as any ticket scalper or metals trader. But anyone plying their trade as a pop star can at least be proud of their product as long as the dynamic pricing is kept at bay. Be it a squillion-selling number-one hit single or a Mixolydian-mode cantata for voice, crumhorn and Paraguayan nose-flute that sells well in Godalming, the art of Terpsichore is sure to please a middling-to-massive chunk of the spending classes. The problem sets in when rock stars, in fits of exceptionalism, decide their wealth and the manner of its accumulation is morally superior to any other. Like, say, Adele or LeBron James, Chrissie Hynde might have brought more pleasure to more people than the more cynical business magnate, but the sports/entertainment dollar still comes tainted with exploitation.

Over Blair's galloping tom-toms and Billy's McGuinn-like guitar, Chrissie reverbs and yelps her way through a lyric that feels stuck to the tongue she has firmly in her cheek. 'We slash their tyres 'cause we're pathetic, and we get paid for the repairs by the millionaires!' she trills, investing the song with as much tacit censure of the great unwashed as she holds in reserve for the obscenely rich, even if she – loosely – aligns herself more with the former. But there's many a truer word spoken in taking the piss, and 'Millionaires' can just about scrape by on the 'satire' or 'social commentary' ticket, although it's a close-run thing.

'May This Be Love' 2:43 (Hendrix)
The Pretenders follow the previous album's 'Room Full Of Mirrors' with another Jimi Hendrix cover. It's another of the maestro's less well-travelled songs, a beautiful ballad from *Are You Experienced?* in which Jimi took time out from the lysergic ferocity of that peerless 1967 debut and created a tender paean to a mythic entity. 'Waterfall', who gave the song its original title, was a Native American ocean goddess and one facet of the part-Cherokee guitarist's romanticised ideal of womanhood. The Pretenders give a suitably respectful, laid-back reading, as luminous guitars from Tchad Blake and Billy Bremner pare back the master's original glissando colourings, allowing in a single arpeggio at 1.00 as a reminder of the grace notes with which Jimi sonically described his ethereal subject.

While superficially The Pretenders' version of 'May This Be Love' offers little of the resonance and acid import of 'Room Full Of Mirrors', this makes as much sense as any of the obvious potential Hendrix covers. Chrissie Hynde understood how much more there was to the alpha stud who, as the epitome of strutting rock 'n' roll sexuality, had so helped shape her youth and her development as a musician. Part of those formative years would have been enlivened by bedroom-wall avatars of the idealised rock god of modern myth. An archetype not known for shrinking-violet tendencies in dealing with the opposite sex, he was personified by Jimi Hendrix. However, songs such as 'May This Be Love', 'The Wind Cries Mary', 'Angel', 'Little Wing' and 'Bold As Love' (the latter of which will become The Pretenders' third Hendrix cover, included on the collaborative *Stone Free: A Tribute To Jimi Hendrix* in 1993) proved that the potency and self-belief of rock's ultimate wild man were tempered with a vulnerability not always evident in the heavy, whitebread blues/rock of the late 1960s. From Clapton to Page and beyond, most of Jimi's macho brother axemen were more concerned with amping up the shot-my-woman-down folklore of the Mississippi Delta than with pausing to see who might be offended. The Pretenders could have taken the same easy route with a by-rote retelling of 'Foxy Lady', 'Stone Free' or 'Hey Joe' (Jimi's own slice of misogynist outlaw gothic was already a garage standby; having made Billy Roberts' song famous, and with it the Hendrix brand, the guitarist soon became keen to disown it). While there's no question that The Pretenders would have made a fine fist of those and other chauvinist classics, Chrissie instead channels Jimi's sensitive, epicene side, demonstrating kinship with a subtle, dreamlike femininity that a strident sisterhood – who'd *so* love to have gotten her on board at the time – might find a tad too spiritual and unworldly. Coming from the woman many might regard as the ultimate swaggering rock chick, the oestrogen Jim Morrison if not Jimi Hendrix, it's a doubly nice touch.

'No Guarantee' 3:47 (Hynde)

If Chrissie is ground down by defeatism elsewhere on *Packed!*, one of the album's most upbeat songs does a good job of dispersing the uncertainties. Far from the fretful doubts of 'Never Do That' and 'Let's Make A Pact', the message of 'No Guarantee' is uncompromising: according to the warranty in question, no-one in the company of Chrissie Hynde, whether as a party-going companion, sexual partner or even a Pretenders concert attendee, can expect automatic right of return if the product isn't what it says on the tin. Instead she demands her own terms, albeit some targeted at a niche market: 'Oh guarantee when you're coming in me you got a rubber on baby', she insists, a stipulation her imprudent younger self would have been less likely to impose ten years before. In places, she concedes that no guarantee will afford her, or anybody else, a buffer against the extravagant expectations of others, the ravages of time or even the immediately, destructively hedonistic. Like all the usual fine-print Ts & Cs, her requirements are ambiguous:

> Guarantee me for a month of good Sundays
> Promise me every single one'll be fun days
> Give me a dime for every party revolution
> Launder my debts in paragorical [sic] solution
> Even the boss has been slandered and slagged
> Now he's sitting in the alley with a bottle in a paper bag.

A paregoric is a 4% tincture of opium: a hearty brew that also contains anise oil, camphor, benzoic acid and, in some forms, belladonna. Its reference here reminds us of the world Chrissie inhabits, no matter how much maturity, motherhood and new-found modesty will attempt to distance her from it. The singer reminds us that this is a fickle wasteland of broken dreams and promises, one that will spit out and discard 'even the boss'. Here the boss could be a fallen idol, anyone who's dallied with rock 'n' roll's lethal acclaim and not made it out the other side. Do we again detect the appearance of Jimi Hendrix in an unbilled cameo? Elsewhere she notes that not every gig is certain of a full house, or at least of much life beyond the theatre's 17th row. It's an acknowledgement, for the time being at least, that The Pretenders' star is dimmed in comparison with the fiery white dwarf of 1978:

> No guarantee
> When we play
> Turn the house lights up Bob
> Fellas look over there

This hall is empty
Yeah, yeah, yeah
Up to 17B
But what's depressing
Oh, oh, oh, whoa, whoa, whoa, whoa
No guarantee, yeah.

The terms of the various deals are set out beneath a frantic few minutes of crotch-clutching rock 'n' roll. In part it's 'Bad Boys Get Spanked', in part Love's 'My Little Red Book'. With Froom's keyboards sliding intermittently around the stanzas like little glowworms, the middle eight at 1.10 floods back in around a minute before the close, solidifying into a sturdy wall of sound erected by no less than three chiming leads. Besides Tchad Blake and Billy Bremner, the sleeve credits Chrissie with guitar, presumably in addition to her duties on rhythm that are usually taken as read. She hawks out her vocal with breathless fury, brooking no dissent and anxious to make her case, no matter how oblique. Just how we like it, then.

'When Will I See You' 4:53 (Hynde/Johnny Marr)
'When Will I See You' is another instance of Chrissie Hynde venturing into the middle of the road. So far, we feel, that The Pretenders risk being flattened by the conveys of grunge, house and dance barrelling towards them in the other direction. Despite Froom's diligently pristine production, the usual great playing and the presence of Johnny Marr as co-composer, the song feels more like a by-the-numbers exercise in writing for the day's hitmakers than a worthwhile addition to The Pretenders' canon: a body of work that, as we've seen, effortlessly combines rock 'n' roll music of light and shade, lyrical sass and sensitivity and a shrewd nose for the business end of pop. ('Sense Of Purpose', which nimbly follows the fractured 'When Will I See You' and manages to pick up some of the pieces, is as good an example of the band's preferred way of doing things as any the late 1980s can offer.)

Despite Tim Finn, Mark Hart and Chrissie cooing saccharine backing vocals in the choruses, the featherlight arrangement of 'When Will I See You' is actually far from unpleasant, with stirring block chords from Bremner (or possibly Hynde) providing a satisfying middle lift at 2.17 and later at 3.58. Unfortunately any wistful tenderness and vulnerability, surely the song's *raisons d'être*, are severely compromised by an uncharacteristically clichéd approach to lyric writing. Meanwhile couplets that once wouldn't have made it past a first draft give oxygen to the notion that Chrissie assembled these weary sentiments from a gift set, then tied them with a bow for the first buyer.

'Sense Of Purpose' 3:03 (Hynde)
Without question one of the album's best moments, 'Sense Of Purpose' proves that Chrissie's ear for a hit tune remains unimpeachable. Not to be confused

with namesake songs by the Sound, the Pop Group or Third World, 'Sense Of Purpose' is irresistibly commercial, pitched squarely at chart success. This would be erratic, however; unreleased in the UK, the single limped to a purposeless number 129 in Australia but fared better in the USA, where it reached number 23 on *Billboard* Alt.

The gated reverb makes a return to the mix, but doesn't quite despoil the toe-tappingly strummed rhythm, liquid guitars and memorable melody. But again the lyrics suggest self-doubt, as Chrissie makes her pitch to an unknown suitor. Though she's in her prime, she has no faith in her own natural vigour, obliged to convince him verbally how much his life will be enriched as long as she's there. Take me home, she pleads, bigging herself up as a formidable lover and partner to a quarry she perceives as outgunning even her:

I'm potent, baby, I'm potent
Just one swing of me would get most guys smashed
But a drop of yours makes me stagger and swerve
I guess I'm outclassed.

While tacitly she concedes that taking her on is not for the fainthearted, her power seemingly does not match his. Once again, Chrissie reduces herself to the supine character whose petticoats have occasionally enshrouded even this predatory virago. It's almost as if she's mildly embarrassed by a public persona that's nonetheless in her blood, with neither confection nor pretence. Once more she touches base with one James Marshall Hendrix, who, with awful consequences, was crushed by an image multiplied by acid and then overcooked and consumed by the recording industry. Her doubts accord with the tenor of the whole album, even if 'Sense Of Purpose' couches them in pop magic.

As for the object of her desire, for once he's admirably civilised. He's the 'new man' whom advertisers at the turn of the 1990s identified as the exemplar of modern masculinity. 'Bully boys don't bother me', she insists, while 'guys like you who are gentle and true don't come around here every day.' Not a Nazi dagger in sight, then.

The singer's taste for a fellow with a reasonably well-attuned feminine side appeared to be missed by the director Mary Lambert, who made the promo vid for 'Sense Of Purpose'. The movie features Chrissie the militant veggie for once getting behind the beefcake. A tough-guy 'love-interest', light-middleweight boxer Gary Stretch, exhibits his extreme sense of purpose by tenderising a human-punchbag opponent in a title fight. Meanwhile Chrissie cheers Gary on at ringside, for the purposes of this deeply strange film clearly in awe of Neanderthal gladiators pounding each other into hamburger. The video, as much a promotional vehicle for the sometime actor and model Stretch as for The Pretenders, is again shot in mono, but at least it takes a stab at a narrative, albeit a violently sweaty one. Whether the story is as appetising as the song is a matter of taste.

'Downtown (Akron)' 2:43 (Hynde)
Once again Chrissie returns to her old Ohio feeding grounds. She tells us nothing new, but it doesn't matter, for the spirit that moves the song's protagonist and her crew is the same that relocated a certain young Akron native to London in 1973 to form a kicking rock 'n' roll band.

'Downtown (Akron)' is a fast, stuttering, amyl nitrite-fuelled starshell, the aural equivalent of copping off in a back alley with a gangbanger packing his pink slip from Firestone and a switchblade. Of all the songs on this curate's egg of an album, this may well be closest to the old Pretenders ideal: 'Meet me in a fire fight, of lusty boys and candlelight', she raps, as she moves to the heart of the city and her 'veins pop and cry for more'. Once again she issues an explicit instruction to the homie hoping to carve another notch into his studded belt: 'Rubber glove me when you love me, promise me protection,' she demands not unreasonably, as the Heavy Bikers bear down on Akron's storied Portage Hotel and the Cuyahoga Valley. She enjoins her companion to 'Downtown me with a lobotomy... and make a man of me', as if recalling a tomboyish younger self who took shit from no-one.

The concave self-pity of the earlier part of *Packed!* now gives way to a nihilist's urge to self-destruct – emotionally, physically, sexually – reminiscent of Chrissie's mindset when she armed the opening four-song salvo of *Pretenders*. Even the structure of 'Downtown (Akron)' harks back to the days when she'd crowbar in her lyrics, irrespective of whether they'd logistically fit the tune or initiate a collective fit of the vapours among the rhythm section. Reeking of Bud, 'ludes, White Lightnin', sump oil, stale Winstons and even staler long-term expectations, 'Downtown (Akron)' is a dishonourably malodorous addition to Chrissie's compendium of hometown street poetry, while saying nothing new. Except, perhaps, to remind us that Akron, the windswept high noon of post-industrial America, indirectly spawned The Pretenders, their leader one of its greatest exports.

'How Do I Miss You' 4:21 (Hynde)
This is another in The Pretenders' series of occasional light brushes with reggae. Chrissie ditches acidic sexual politics ('Private Life') and worthy eco-activism ('Waste Not Want Not') to discuss bittersweet emotional themes under a honied, tearful helping of lovers' rock. In places, 'How Do I Miss You' is baffling in typically Hyndeian fashion. Once again this is no conventional love song, but an autumnal, minor-key rumination on the complex vagaries of life that permit or thwart the success of a close, if passing relationship.

The unequivocal intro lines set out the singer's acute feelings of loss following a departure. Chrissie's recent songwriting history isn't exactly free of maudlin sentimentality. On first hearing, fears begin to simmer over another song that might drift towards self-pity, and the over-familiar sense that she is resigning herself to helplessness. However, have faith – after all, this *is* Chrissie Hynde. Her every song, be its topic sex, breakup, fur coats or the most flak-free flightpath for a surgical raid on Burger King, cannot be judged on every lyrical misstep of the recent past. Any more than *Packed!* may coolly be dismissed as a viable Pretenders album because glossy production values are apparently at odds with an earlier model.

Sure enough, the circumstances attending the singer's mood soon become satisfyingly foggy, as Chrissie attempts to elucidate how the departee (a 'silly Welsh git', apparently) was:

> Sold down the river
> Like a slave changing hands
> From master to master
> The leaves will turn brown
> And fall to the ground
> And another summer is gone
> Gone is the summer of you, oh.

The closest clue to her mindset when she wrote 'How Do I Miss You' arrives in the second verse. If at the beginning of the relationship she was less than serious, almost contemptuously so, the inevitable exit of her lover is hard to bear. Ruefully she figures out how much she misses someone she was a little too quick to feign indifference towards:

> It got so when I looked at you
> I did it for a laugh
> Now your laughter fills the room
> When I'm trying to take a bath
> When the chorus of the dawn
> Fills the valley with song
> Baby what could be wrong
> My heart is breaking in two, oh.

The singer's uncertainty builds as she thinly qualifies the Caribbean-style arrangement and finds herself 'walking down the street to the carnival beat, but I'm dragging my feet, because I'm hopelessly blue'. At the risk of overdoing the Jimi Hendrix references in this appraisal of The Pretenders' music, is this love, or confusion? Chrissie seems to be compacting numerous disparate feelings into the same song. It's like the first draft of a stream of consciousness that she'll refine just as soon as she's gathered her thoughts over a shot or two. But isn't this what heartache is about? Who can honestly say they can qualify and quantify their immediate emotional response to unexpected loss – and one worries that Chrissie was suddenly kicked into touch by this severe personal setback – as her feelings fall over themselves and her hormones do handsprings?

Musically the song does a dub-lite take on Joseph Hill and Joe Gibbs' roots-reggae group Culture, with beautifully economic guitar lines from Billy Bremner sneaking around Tony Gad's forthright bass and eddying Hammond from Mitchell Froom. Like much of the rest of *Packed!*, 'How Do I Miss You' is a grower, sitting nicely on the album between the relative exuberance of the songs before and after it, suggesting that the instincts that so judiciously programmed The Pretenders' albums since the heady days of 1979 are, contrary to received wisdom, still alive and kicking.

'Hold A Candle To This' 3:37 (Hynde)

At one or more live gigs of the time, Chrissie Hynde dedicated 'Hold A Candle To This' to 'all you meat-eaters out there that have turned this country into a slaughterhouse'. Thereby she demonstrated the depth of her recall from the public-relations classes that probably weren't taught at Kent State.

For the most part, 'Hold A Candle To This' is about the near-lifelong vegetarian taking potshots at the accursed fatstock industry. But there's a sense that Chrissie's charge sheet asks for numerous other offences, committed by a raft of bogeymen, to be taken into consideration. From a First Lady armed and dangerous in the White House Residence (in 1980, Nancy Reagan admitted to *The New York Times* that she stowed a 'tiny little gun' in a bedside drawer, and that her cowpoke hubby President Ron had shown her how to use it) to priapic US Navy sailors fathering several new nations whenever they disembarked in Osaka, Siam and Saigon, a host of bad actors are set up ready for Chrissie to mow down with extreme prejudice.

It's nice to hear the album-wide melancholy hasn't completely subsumed Chrissie's usual fury, which she compresses into one of *Packed!*'s better sets of lyrics. She frames them in an arrangement muscular enough to have felt at home even on the pugnacious *Learning To Crawl*. Yet while the messaging is sometimes messy and unfocused, Chrissie maintains a wry sense of levity, cooling the anger rather than reducing it to the point where nothing hits home.

Sometimes, however, we're reminded of Chrissie's infamous McDonald's intervention, a jape that backfired despite the professed element of coincidence. Shouldn't the instruction embedded in 'Hold A Candle To This' to 'Blow up the abattoir, detonate!' only be taken seriously when uttered by certain revolutionary rentagobs of the late-1960s counterculture? It's something that Wolfie Smith, Robert Lindsay's hapless workers' anti-hero from the 1970s UK sitcom, *Citizen Smith* might say. Surely it's far too absurdly, theatrically jarring and agitprop for a smart, sceptical writer such as Chrissie Hynde, but perhaps she was joking at all those live gigs, too.

'Criminal' 3:49 (Hynde)

The Pretenders duly obey the convention of closing out a suite of songs with something elegiac, even if the sentiments of 'Criminal' are too suspiciously negative to deliver an uplifting finale. At least the final track on *Packed!* aligns with the black mood elsewhere. 'Criminal' is musically plaintive, not unlike 'I Go To Sleep' in flavour. It's tempting to identify the author of that song as the ex-lover to whom Chrissie here addresses another epistle of tearfulness. She may be lamenting her relationship with Ray Davies six years after the pair finished. Chrissie surely is reminded of Ray and of better times past whenever she plays with their daughter, Natalie, or on those occasions *that* photo falls accidentally from her wallet. Assuming 'Criminal' is indeed a *roman-à-clef*, be it related to Ray, Jim or anybody else, Chrissie clearly feels the loss:

> You made me some kind of criminal
> You put me outlaw, because I loved you
> The first thing I think when I wake up – when can I see you?
> The last thing I think when I'm drifting off – when will I see you?
> Oh look at me, I'm addicted still
> At first I refused – now I just swallow the pill
> Baby, won't you fix me like you used to?

Yet again Chrissie bypasses her old take-no-prisoners belligerence for meek and passive capitulation. She's willing to shoulder the blame for whatever killed off this relationship, painting herself less a victim of love, fate or corrosive predilections, more the helpless patsy whose miscalculation brought it all tumbling down upon herself, with no defence in law. Even if it's his fault, it's still her fault, just as she goaded her bad-boy nemesis from 'Up The Neck' into measuring her up for that lamp cord, or so irradiated with passion were the Tattooed Love Boys they simply couldn't help themselves when they raped her in their clubroom. Such a sense of guilt can be almost Jesuit in its misguided conviction. In an attempt to cleanse herself of shame, she mercilessly self-flagellates.

This is heartfelt stuff, to be sure. Even if Chrissie's angst is misplaced and she has nothing, in reality, to beat herself up about, here is a songwriter committing a bad time in her life to trenchant and abrasive poetry. Or, to play devil's advocate, it's a consummate professional at her craft, silkscreening glib, carefully manicured words to order – although no-one could ever accuse Chrissie Hynde of being Gilbert O'Sullivan. Either way, and despite a glistering arrangement as appealing as any on *Packed!*, the bleak and downbeat sentiments of 'Criminal' provide a strangely suitable valediction to an album that's very much better than it tries to be.

Associated
Bonus Tracks Included With 2015 CD Reissue Of Packed!
'Not A Second Time' 2:11 (Lennon/McCartney)
Few have lost credibility or their shirts covering a Beatles tune or two. The trick is to ensure due deference is paid to the people who started it all, and if you're going to upset the applecart, make sure it's à la Spooky Tooth's 'I Am

The Walrus' or Joe Cocker's similarly radicalised 'With A Little Help From My Friends'. Doffing their own titfers with the utmost respect, The Pretenders lobbed their version of a less obvious, but no less wonderful, Fabs song from 1963's *With The Beatles* onto the B-side of the 'Sense Of Purpose' single. They play a straight bat. James Honeyman-Scott would have approved.

'Spirit Of Life' 4.09 (Meg Keene)
CD bandwidths being much broader than old 45rpm vinyl meant a single, in 1990, was more like an EP in 1964. Perhaps that's why 'Spirit Of Life' found itself bundled in with 'Sense Of Purpose'. Chrissie tosses Meg Keene more useful royalties, although the single's performance – unplaced in the UK, it made only number 23 on *Billboard*'s Alt chart – was hardly that of 'Brass In Pocket', paradoxically also included. But with her old high-school pal's poetic words cossetted in another shimmeringly exquisite arrangement, beautifully produced by Mitchell Froom, the fact that the record generally tanked seems, er, criminal.

Postscript

Four years after the fine music, great production yet frequently downbeat sentiments of *Packed!*, Chrissie Hynde re-upped The Pretenders with bassist Andy Hobson (formerly with The Primitives) and guitarist Adam Seymour (ex-Katydids). She also brought Martin Chambers back in from the cold, as she told *Hot Press* in 1994:

> I missed [Martin] terribly. Both he and I were floundering – and probably not playing well – and I need someone to kick me in the ass and inspire me. We went through one song and it was the same buzz as when we first played together. No-one has that swing and feel.

Reconvened, happy and with Ian Stanley now at the studio desk, The Pretenders came bouncing back with the excellent *Last Of The Independents*, which reached number eight in the UK and number 41 in the States. In 1995, the same lineup (plus guest pianist Damon Albarn) released a live album taped from a TV show, *The Isle Of View* (23 and 100 respectively), in which the motorcycle gang with guitars proved they could share a stage with a string quartet without class warfare breaking out. The performance also provided definitive evidence of how seamlessly Chrissie's classic songs (including, among others, 'The Phone Call', 'Private Life', 'Chill Factor' and 'Lovers Of Today') could pass the voltage test and transition from electric to mainly acoustic. 1999 saw another superb studio album, *¡Viva El Amor!* (32 and an incomprehensible 158), one track of which found the now stabilised quartet augmented by the guitarist Chrissie literally had once wanted to be, Jeff Beck.

In 1997, Chrissie married Colombian artist Lucho Brieva. The pair separated in 2002. Three years later, The Pretenders were inducted into the Rock & Roll Hall of Fame. As befitted the originals and best, Chrissie and Martin were the only band members to attend the ceremony, but afterwards Adam and Andy joined the old-timers onstage to perform 'Precious' and 'Message Of Love'. Accepting the award, Chrissie wryly named and thanked everyone who'd nominally been a Pretender since the beginning:

> I know that The Pretenders have looked like a tribute band for the last 20 years ... and we're paying tribute to James Honeyman-Scott and Pete Farndon, without whom we wouldn't be here. And on the other hand, without us, they might have been here, but that's the way it works in rock 'n' roll.

Despite – or, in some cases, because of – the anguish of the early 1980s, Chrissie's songs have frequently projected values that are more traditional than those of many rock stars. As we have seen, she's even occasionally excused her ill-treatment at the hands of a succession of bad boys as if she, not they, were to blame: a position that likely had more than a few right-on activists baying for her blood. Doubling down in a 2006 *Billboard* interview, Chrissie adamantly denied she was a feminist. Today, as always the contrarian reversing a time-worn supposition – in this instance, that getting older inescapably begets a safe, reactionary conservatism – she's circled back, happier to wave the flag for women's rights than she's ever been, as she assured *The Guardian* in 2023: 'I think I'm a poster girl for feminism. There's nothing about me that is not feminist, through and through.'

If Chrissie is glad at last to take one for the sisterhood, she's continued to fight the good fight against animal testing and the fur trade. In 2000, she and three associates were arrested in connection with trashing $1,000 worth of black-market leather at a New York branch of Gap. The case was dismissed after she pledged to stay out of trouble for six months. Four years later she led a protest in France against KFC. Meanwhile in 2013, Natalie Hynde made her mother proud when she was arrested for attaching herself to a fracking site drill.

Today, Chrissie has detoxed from the pernicious addictions that killed her two cherished friends and bandmates and almost destroyed her band. Booze, dope, even cigarettes – all are history. During Pretenders hiatuses, she lives quietly at her studio home in Maida Vale, north London, writing and painting abstracts, portraits and landscapes. From time to time, she bumps into her neighbour and fellow artist, Ron Wood; perhaps the pair meet for coffee and recount a certain youthful encounter in a Cleveland hotel. She published a compendium of 200 of her paintings, *Adding The Blue*, in 2018. Retaining her long-held dual UK-US citizenship alongside less bureaucratic links with her past, she also owns an apartment in Northside Lofts, Akron.

At time of writing, Chrissie is preparing the band for an autumn 2024 UK tour, following a hastily-announced but triumphant set at Glastonbury 2023 in which The Pretenders of the moment – Chrissie, James Walbourne (guitar), Kris Sonne (drums) and Dave Page (bass) – were joined onstage by Johnny Marr and fellow Ohioan Dave Grohl, with even a hug and an avuncular thumbs-up from the wings courtesy of Paul McCartney. Sidelined once more, however, was Martin Chambers, who later complained to *MusicRadar* that he 'couldn't be bothered with all the aggro Chrissie gives me.' After playing on The Pretenders' 2002 album *Loose Screw*, the drummer worked with McCartney, Mick Ronson and Dave Stewart & The Spiritual Cowboys, returning to his old muckers for *Hate For Sale* in 2020. In 2017, Martin announced he was writing a memoir, *The Last Pretender*, whose publication presumably hinges on the prevailing state of one of rock's most enduring and confusing love-hate relationships.

Back in Akron, the depressed economy of 2011 forced Chrissie to withdraw from her own labour of love: a critically acclaimed vegan restaurant in her home town called The VegiTerranean. Two years earlier, she contributed to *Cows And The Earth: A Story Of Kinder Dairy Farming*, a book that combined her Vaishnavism with her beliefs in vegetarianism and compassionate farming. She now supports a dairy farm in Rutland, UK, which is run according to Brahmanist *ahimsa* principles of refraining from killing or harming living creatures.

Spirituality continues to percolate through Christine Ellen Hynde's life and art. In 2023, her old friend and one-time landlord, the filmmaker Don Letts, asked her what she believes is the purpose of music. She replied:

> For me, it's a matter of divinity. It's a way of connecting us with the supreme and finding a sort of self-realisation. If you hear birds singing in the morning, that's maybe the purest form of it. Music awakens the spirit.

Also available from Sonicbond

On Track series
AC/DC – Chris Sutton 978-1-78952-307-2
Allman Brothers Band – Andrew Wild 978-1-78952-252-5
Tori Amos – Lisa Torem 978-1-78952-142-9
Aphex Twin – Beau Waddell 978-1-78952-267-9
Asia – Peter Braidis 978-1-78952-099-6
Badfinger – Robert Day-Webb 978-1-878952-176-4
Barclay James Harvest – Keith and Monica Domone 978-1-78952-067-5
Beck – Arthur Lizie 978-1-78952-258-7
The Beat, General Public, Fine Young Cannibals – Steve Parry 978-1-78952-274-7
The Beatles 1962-1996 – Alberto Bravin and Andrew Wild 978-1-78952-355-3
The Beatles Solo 1969-1980 – Andrew Wild 978-1-78952-030-9
Blue Oyster Cult – Jacob Holm-Lupo 978-1-78952-007-1
Blur – Matt Bishop 978-178952-164-1
Marc Bolan and T.Rex – Peter Gallagher 978-1-78952-124-5
David Bowie 1964 to 1982 – Carl Ewens 978-1-78952-324-9
David Bowie 1963 to 2016 – Don Klees 978-1-78952-351-5
Kate Bush – Bill Thomas 978-1-78952-097-2
The Byrds – Andy McArthur 978-1-78952-280-8
Camel – Hamish Kuzminski 978-1-78952-040-8
Captain Beefheart – Opher Goodwin 978-1-78952-235-8
Caravan – Andy Boot 978-1-78952-127-6
Cardiacs – Eric Benac 978-1-78952-131-3
Wendy Carlos – Mark Marrington 978-1-78952-331-7
The Carpenters – Paul Tornbohm 978-1-78952-301-0
Nick Cave and The Bad Seeds – Dominic Sanderson 978-1-78952-240-2
Eric Clapton Solo – Andrew Wild 978-1-78952-141-2
The Clash (revised edition) – Nick Assirati 978-1-78952-325-6
Elvis Costello and The Attractions – Georg Purvis 978-1-78952-129-0
Crosby, Stills and Nash – Andrew Wild 978-1-78952-039-2
Creedence Clearwater Revival – Tony Thompson 978-1-78952-237-2
Crowded House – Jon Magidsohn 978-1-78952-292-1
The Damned – Morgan Brown 978-1-78952-136-8
David Bowie 1964 to 1982 – Carl Ewens 978-1-78952-324-9
David Bowie 1964 to 1982 – Carl Ewens 978-1-78952-324-9
Deep Purple and Rainbow 1968-79 – Steve Pilkington 978-1-78952-002-6
Deep Purple from 1984 – Phil Kafcaloudes 978-1-78952-354-6
Depeche Mode – Brian J. Robb 978-1-78952-277-8
Dire Straits – Andrew Wild 978-1-78952-044-6
The Divine Comedy – Alan Draper 978-1-78952-308-9
The Doors – Tony Thompson 978-1-78952-137-5
Dream Theater – Jordan Blum 978-1-78952-050-7
Bob Dylan 1962-1970 – Opher Goodwin 978-1-78952-275-2
Eagles – John Van der Kiste 978-1-78952-260-0
Earth, Wind and Fire – Bud Wilkins 978-1-78952-272-3
Electric Light Orchestra – Barry Delve 978-1-78952-152-8
Emerson Lake and Palmer – Mike Goode 978-1-78952-000-2
Fairport Convention – Kevan Furbank 978-1-78952-051-4
Peter Gabriel – Graeme Scarfe 978-1-78952-138-2
Genesis – Stuart MacFarlane 978-1-78952-005-7
Gentle Giant – Gary Steel 978-1-78952-058-3
Gong – Kevan Furbank 978-1-78952-082-8
Green Day – William E. Spevack 978-1-78952-261-7
Steve Hackett – Geoffrey Feakes 978-1-78952-098-9
Hall and Oates – Ian Abrahams 978-1-78952-162-1
Peter Hammill – Richard Rees Jones 978-1-78952-163-4
Roy Harper – Opher Goodwin 978-1-78952-130-6
Hawkwind (new edition) – Duncan Harris 978-1-78952-290-7
Jimi Hendrix – Emma Stott 978-1-78952-175-7

Also available from Sonicbond

The Hollies – Andrew Darlington 978-1-78952-159-7
Horslips – Richard James 978-1-78952-263-1
The Human League and The Sheffield Scene – Andrew Darlington 978-1-78952-186-3
Humble Pie –Robert Day-Webb 978-1-78952-2761
Ian Hunter – G. Mick Smith 978-1-78952-304-1
The Incredible String Band – Tim Moon 978-1-78952-107-8
INXS – Manny Grillo 978-1-78952-302-7
Iron Maiden – Steve Pilkington 978-1-78952-061-3
Joe Jackson – Richard James 978-1-78952-189-4
The Jam – Stan Jeffries 978-1-78952-299-0
Jefferson Airplane – Richard Butterworth 978-1-78952-143-6
Jethro Tull – Jordan Blum 978-1-78952-016-3
J. Geils Band – James Romag 978-1-78952-332-4
Elton John in the 1970s – Peter Kearns 978-1-78952-034-7
Billy Joel – Lisa Torem 978-1-78952-183-2
Journey – Doug Thornton 978-1-78952-337-9
Judas Priest – John Tucker 978-1-78952-018-7
Kansas – Kevin Cummings 978-1-78952-057-6
Killing Joke – Nic Ransome 978-1-78952-273-0
The Kinks – Martin Hutchinson 978-1-78952-172-6
Korn – Matt Karpe 978-1-78952-153-5
Led Zeppelin – Steve Pilkington 978-1-78952-151-1
Level 42 – Matt Philips 978-1-78952-102-3
Little Feat – Georg Purvis – 978-1-78952-168-9
Magnum – Matthew Taylor – 978-1-78952-286-0
Aimee Mann – Jez Rowden 978-1-78952-036-1
Ralph McTell – Paul O. Jenkins 978-1-78952-294-5
Metallica – Barry Wood 978-1-78952-269-3
Joni Mitchell – Peter Kearns 978-1-78952-081-1
The Moody Blues – Geoffrey Feakes 978-1-78952-042-2
Motorhead – Duncan Harris 978-1-78952-173-3
Nektar – Scott Meze – 978-1-78952-257-0
New Order – Dennis Remmer – 978-1-78952-249-5
Nightwish – Simon McMurdo – 978-1-78952-270-9
Nirvana – William E. Spevack 978-1-78952-318-8
Laura Nyro – Philip Ward 978-1-78952-182-5
Oasis – Andrew Rooney 978-1-78952-300-3
Phil Ochs – Opher Goodwin 978-1-78952-326-3
Mike Oldfield – Ryan Yard 978-1-78952-060-6
Opeth – Jordan Blum 978-1-78-952-166-5
Pearl Jam – Ben L. Connor 978-1-78952-188-7
Tom Petty – Richard James 978-1-78952-128-3
Pink Floyd – Richard Butterworth 978-1-78952-242-6
The Police – Pete Braidis 978-1-78952-158-0
Porcupine Tree (Revised Edition) – Nick Holmes 978-1-78952-346-1
Procol Harum – Scott Meze 978-1-78952-315-7
Queen – Andrew Wild 978-1-78952-003-3
Radiohead – William Allen 978-1-78952-149-8
Gerry Rafferty – John Van der Kiste 978-1-78952-349-2
Rancid – Paul Matts 978-1-78952-187-0
Lou Reed 1972-1986 – Ethan Roy 978-1-78952-283-9
Renaissance – David Detmer 978-1-78952-062-0
REO Speedwagon – Jim Romag 978-1-78952-262-4
The Rolling Stones 1963-80 – Steve Pilkington 978-1-78952-017-0
Linda Ronstadt 1969-1989 – Daryl O. Lawrence 987-1-78952-293-8
Roxy Music – Michael Kulikowski 978-1-78952-335-5
Rush 1973 to 1982 – Richard James 978-1-78952-338-6
Sensational Alex Harvey Band – Peter Gallagher 978-1-7952-289-1
The Small Faces and The Faces – Andrew Darlington 978-1-78952-316-4

Also available from Sonicbond

The Smashing Pumpkins – Matt Karpe 978-1-7952-291-4
The Smiths and Morrissey – Tommy Gunnarsson 978-1-78952-140-5
Soft Machine – Scott Meze 978-1078952-271-6
Sparks 1969-1979 – Chris Sutton 978-1-78952-279-2
Spirit – Rev. Keith A. Gordon – 978-1-78952- 248-8
Stackridge – Alan Draper 978-1-78952-232-7
Status Quo the Frantic Four Years – Richard James 978-1-78952-160-3
Steely Dan – Jez Rowden 978-1-78952-043-9
The Stranglers – Martin Hutchinson 978-1-78952-323-2
Talk Talk – Gary Steel 978-1-78952-284-6
Talking Heads – David Starkey 978-178952-353-9
Tears For Fears – Paul Clark – 978-178952-238-9
Thin Lizzy – Graeme Stroud 978-1-78952-064-4
Tool – Matt Karpe 978-1-78952-234-1
Toto – Jacob Holm-Lupo 978-1-78952-019-4
U2 – Eoghan Lyng 978-1-78952-078-1
UFO – Richard James 978-1-78952-073-6
Ultravox – Brian J. Robb 978-1-78952-330-0
Van Der Graaf Generator – Dan Coffey 978-1-78952-031-6
Van Halen – Morgan Brown – 9781-78952-256-3
Suzanne Vega – Lisa Torem 978-1-78952-281-5
Jack White And The White Stripes – Ben L. Connor 978-1-78952-303-4
The Who – Geoffrey Feakes 978-1-78952-076-7
Roy Wood and the Move – James R Turner 978-1-78952-008-8
Yes (new edition) – Stephen Lambe 978-1-78952-282-2
Neil Young 1963 to 1970 – Oper Goodwin 978-1-78952-298-3
Frank Zappa 1966 to 1979 – Eric Benac 978-1-78952-033-0
Warren Zevon – Peter Gallagher 978-1-78952-170-2
The Zombies – Emma Stott 978-1-78952-297-6
10CC – Peter Kearns 978-1-78952-054-5

Decades Series
The Bee Gees in the 1960s – Andrew Mon Hughes et al 978-1-78952-148-1
The Bee Gees in the 1970s – Andrew Mon Hughes et al 978-1-78952-179-5
Black Sabbath in the 1970s – Chris Sutton 978-1-78952-171-9
Britpop – Peter Richard Adams and Matt Pooler 978-1-78952-169-6
Phil Collins in the 1980s – Andrew Wild 978-1-78952-185-6
Alice Cooper in the 1970s – Chris Sutton 978-1-78952-104-7
Alice Cooper in the 1980s – Chris Sutton 978-1-78952-259-4
Curved Air in the 1970s – Laura Shenton 978-1-78952-069-9
Donovan in the 1960s – Jeff Fitzgerald 978-1-78952-233-4
Bob Dylan in the 1980s – Don Klees 978-1-78952-157-3
Brian Eno in the 1970s – Gary Parsons 978-1-78952-239-6
Faith No More in the 1990s – Matt Karpe 978-1-78952-250-1
Fleetwood Mac in the 1970s – Andrew Wild 978-1-78952-105-4
Fleetwood Mac in the 1980s – Don Klees 978-178952-254-9
Focus in the 1970s – Stephen Lambe 978-1-78952-079-8
Free and Bad Company in the 1970s – John Van der Kiste 978-1-78952-178-8
Genesis in the 1970s – Bill Thomas 978178952-146-7
George Harrison in the 1970s – Eoghan Lyng 978-1-78952-174-0
Kiss in the 1970s – Peter Gallagher 978-1-78952-246-4
Manfred Mann's Earth Band in the 1970s – John Van der Kiste 978178952-243-3
Marillion in the 1980s – Nathaniel Webb 978-1-78952-065-1
Van Morrison in the 1970s – Peter Childs – 978-1-78952-241-9
Mott the Hoople & Ian Hunter in the 1970s – John Van der Kiste 978-1-78-952-162-7
Pink Floyd In The 1970s – Georg Purvis 978-1-78952-072-9
Suzi Quatro in the 1970s – Darren Johnson 978-1-78952-236-5
Queen in the 1970s – James Griffiths 978-1-78952-265-5
Roxy Music in the 1970s – Dave Thompson 978-1-78952-180-1

Also available from Sonicbond

Slade in the 1970s – Darren Johnson 978-1-78952-268-6
Status Quo in the 1980s – Greg Harper 978-1-78952-244-0
Tangerine Dream in the 1970s – Stephen Palmer 978-1-78952-161-0
The Sweet in the 1970s – Darren Johnson 978-1-78952-139-9
Uriah Heep in the 1970s – Steve Pilkington 978-1-78952-103-0
Van der Graaf Generator in the 1970s – Steve Pilkington 978-1-78952-245-7
Rick Wakeman in the 1970s – Geoffrey Feakes 978-1-78952-264-8
Yes in the 1980s – Stephen Lambe with David Watkinson 978-1-78952-125-2

Rock Classics Series
90125 by Yes – Stephen Lambe 978-1-78952-329-4
Bat Out Of Hell by Meatloaf – Geoffrey Feakes 978-1-78952-320-1
Bringing It All Back Home by Bob Dylan – Opher Goodwin 978-1-78952-314-0
Californication by Red Hot Chili Peppers - Matt Karpe 978-1-78952-348-5
Crime Of The Century by Supertramp – Steve Pilkington 978-1-78952-327-0
The Dreaming by Kate Bush – Peter Kearns 978-1-78952-341-6
Let It Bleed by The Rolling Stones – John Van der Kiste 978-1-78952-309-6
Pawn Hearts by Van Der Graaf Generator – Paolo Carnelli 978-1-78952-357-7
Purple Rain by Prince – Matt Karpe 978-1-78952-322-5
The White Album by The Beatles – Opher Goodwin 978-1-78952-333-1

On Screen Series
Carry On… – Stephen Lambe 978-1-78952-004-0
David Cronenberg – Patrick Chapman 978-1-78952-071-2
Doctor Who: The David Tennant Years – Jamie Hailstone 978-1-78952-066-8
James Bond – Andrew Wild 978-1-78952-010-1
Monty Python – Steve Pilkington 978-1-78952-047-7
Seinfeld Seasons 1 to 5 – Stephen Lambe 978-1-78952-012-5

Other Books
1967: A Year In Psychedelic Rock 978-1-78952-155-9
1970: A Year In Rock – John Van der Kiste 978-1-78952-147-4
1972: The Year Progressive Rock Ruled The World – Kevan Furbank 978-1-78952-288-4
1973: The Golden Year of Progressive Rock 978-1-78952-165-8
Eric Clapton Sessions – Andrew Wild 978-1-78952-177-1
Dark Horse Records – Aaron Badgley 978-1-78952-287-7
Derek Taylor: For Your Radioactive Children – Andrew Darlington 978-1-78952-038-5
Ghosts – Journeys To Post-Pop – Matthew Restall 978-1-78952-334-8
The Golden Age of Easy Listening – Derek Taylor 978-1-78952-285-3
The Golden Road: The Recording History of The Grateful Dead – John Kilbride 978-1-78952-156-6
Hoggin' The Page – Groudhogs The Classic Years – Martyn Hanson 978-1-78952-343-0
Iggy and The Stooges On Stage 1967-1974 – Per Nilsen 978-1-78952-101-6
Jon Anderson and the Warriors – the Road to Yes – David Watkinson 978-1-78952-059-0
Magic: The David Paton Story – David Paton 978-1-78952-266-2
Misty: The Music of Johnny Mathis – Jakob Baekgaard 978-1-78952-247-1
Musical Guide To Red By King Crimson – Andrew Keeling 978-1-78952-321-8
Nu Metal: A Definitive Guide – Matt Karpe 978-1-78952-063-7
Philip Lynott – Renegade – Alan Byrne 978-1-78952-339-3
Remembering Live Aid – Andrew Wild 978-1-78952-328-7
Thank You For The Days - Fans Of The Kinks Share 60 Years of Stories – Ed. Chris Kocher 978-1-78952-342-3
The Sonicbond On Track Sampler – 978-1-78952-190-0
The Sonicbond Progressive Rock Sampler (Ebook only) – 978-1-78952-056-9
Tommy Bolin: In and Out of Deep Purple – Laura Shenton 978-1-78952-070-5
Maximum Darkness – Deke Leonard 978-1-78952-048-4
The Twang Dynasty – Deke Leonard 978-1-78952-049-1

… and many more to come!

Would you like to write for Sonicbond Publishing?

We are mainly a music publisher, but we also occasionally publish in other genres including film and television. At Sonicbond Publishing we are always on the look-out for authors, particularly for our two main series, On Track and Decades.

Mixing fact with in depth analysis, the On Track series examines the entire recorded work of a particular musical artist or group. All genres are considered from easy listening and jazz to 60s soul to 90s pop, via rock and metal.

The Decades series singles out a particular decade in an artist or group's history and focuses on that decade in more detail than may be allowed in the On Track series.

While professional writing experience would, of course, be an advantage, the most important qualification is to have real enthusiasm and knowledge of your subject. First-time authors are welcomed, but the ability to write well in English is essential.

Sonicbond Publishing has distribution throughout Europe and North America, and all our books are also published in E-book form. Authors will be paid a royalty based on sales of their book. Further details about our books are available from www.sonicbondpublishing.com. To contact us, complete the contact form there or email info@sonicbondpublishing.co.uk